CURIOSITIES

OF

CHESHIRE

CURIOSITIES

OF
CHESHIRE

ROBERT NICHOLLS

The
History
Press

To Sylvia, my sister

First published 2010

The History Press
The Mill, Brimscombe Port
Stroud, Gloucestershire, GL5 2QG
www.thehistorypress.co.uk

Reprinted in 2011, 2012

British Library Cataloguing in Publication Data.
A catalogue record for this book is available from the British Library.

ISBN 978 0 7524 5294 4

Typesetting and origination by The History Press
Printed in Great Britain

Contents

ACKNOWLEDGEMENTS

Books of this nature can only be written with the willing assistance of a great number of people. Much information has been garnered from visits to public libraries at Chester, Stockport, Warrington, Wythenshawe and Wilmslow and from the County Record Office at Chester. The pages of other books, guidebooks, the internet, tourist and publicity material produced over the years have also been useful sources of information, and acknowledgments are due to the various authors who have provided material for adaptation in the book.

Particular attention needs to be drawn to Peter Bamford's *Cheshire Curiosities* of 1992. Some of the curiosities in this book duplicate those he has written about, but both books contain sites not found in the other. Where possible, the opportunity has been taken to update the relevant information.

Innumerable land and property owners need to be thanked for giving me access to their properties, and allowing me to take photographs for the purposes of this book. Special thanks are due to Laurie Morgan for use of the photograph on page 113.

Special thanks are also due to Camilla Legh of Adlington Hall, James Brotherhood, Keith McLaren, Gordon Emery, the Revd Beth Gardner, and to Rob Smith of Halton Borough Council's Parks and Countryside Department for answering queries or helping in other ways. Thanks also to my elder son, Patrick, and my girlfriend Pam Craig, for proof-reading the manuscript.

Matilda Richards at The History Press must be thanked for being such a willing advocate of the project and for helping me to realise it.

ABOUT THE AUTHOR

Robert Nicholls has lived in the North West since 1973, holding various professional positions in local government and other organisations. Born in 1952 in Sheffield, he was educated at High Storrs Grammar School, has a degree in Estate Management from Reading University and is qualified as a chartered surveyor. In 2000, he gained an MBA from Lancaster University.

He is the author of numerous local and transport history books, including *Trafford Park: The First Hundred Years*, *Curiosities of Greater Manchester* and *Curiosities of Merseyside*. As well as contributing articles to magazines, he regularly gives talks to local history societies.

INTRODUCTION

I am often asked what is meant by the term 'curiosity'. It is a valid question, and one that is capable of somewhat different responses. In my case, a 'curiosity' is a building, structure, location or landform that is either rare or unusual architecturally, or is associated with a fascinating story, particularly one that might not have reached the pages of the history books.

Present-day Cheshire is a county of great contrasts. It has urban areas both within its boundaries and those that are part of the fringe suburbs of adjoining conurbations. Equally, it has remote areas well away from the busy routes and tourist destinations. Its quiet lanes are well known to cyclists. It includes parts of the Peak District, other hilly areas around the routes of the Gritstone and Sandstone Trails, the central Cheshire Plain, the Welsh borderlands and the southern end of the Wirral. The historic city of Chester itself cannot be ignored.

The curiosities of the county reflect this variety. There are age-old structures from Neolithic times, Roman and medieval remains, industrial and transport features, and evidence of the work of local aristocrats and eccentrics. The churches of Cheshire are a particular delight; fortunately many of them are open to the public.

There are a number of misconceptions about the county that must be dispelled. The first is that it is a 'boring' county visually. This error stems almost entirely from the experience of travelling along the Cheshire stretch of the M6 motorway. The second is that it is a county with interesting fringes, but a flat and uninteresting centre.

Both of these allegations are completely untrue, as a search for the curiosities revealed in this book will easily reveal. The fringes of the county are themselves interesting, but the Cheshire Plain equals them from the number of curiosities to be found there.

Because of its proximity to the conurbations, Cheshire is a county in transition. Parts of it are where the North's 'Super Rich' live, complete with associated 'LA lifestyle/Cheshire postcode' and 'Surrey's Northern cousin' epithets. Industrial and commercial development, criss-crossing busy motorways and growing suburbanization, add to this invasion of the old landscape.

But beneath the surface, the quality of the county remains – and it *is* one of England's most attractive counties, an assertion well supported by the wide range and quality of the curiosities that can be found within its boundaries. The curiosities contained in this book represent a microcosm of the county's rich history, and each has a story to tell and a part to play in its historical development.

The 'county' referred to in this book is the post-1974 administrative unit. Those seeking curiosities in places such as Cheadle, Stockport, Marple and

Mottram-in-Longdendale should have a look at *Curiosities of Greater Manchester*, whilst those north of Parkgate and Willaston in the Wirral are to be found in *Curiosities of Merseyside*.

The choice of curiosities that follow in these pages is inevitably a personal one, bounded by the availability of publishing space. Readers will, I'm sure, find many others.

Robert Nicholls, 2010

VISITING THE CURIOSITIES

Most of the curiosities listed in this book are not tourist attractions in their own right, but can be seen, externally at least, without paying an admission fee. Many are visible from the public highway or from other freely-accessible areas. A few have interiors, or are located in areas which might require payment of an admission charge. Where access is not possible or advisable, this is made clear in the 'Access' details given in the text.

The curiosities can either be visited singly, or in groups by area. Those in the centre of towns are best visited on foot; others make ideal car outings. Parts of the less populated and more rural areas of the county are not well-endowed with good public transport, so some are best accessed by car. Most can be seen by the less mobile.

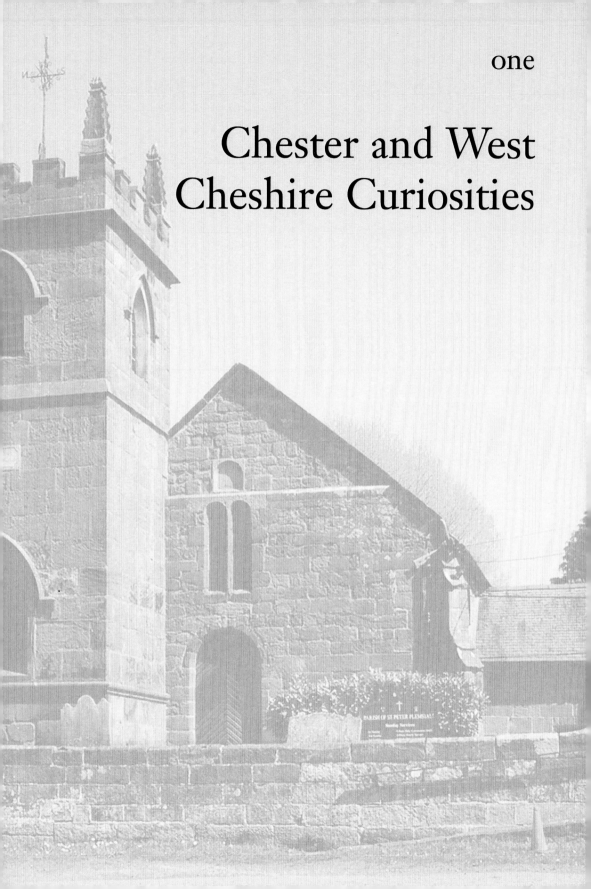

one

Chester and West Cheshire Curiosities

CHESTER'S UNIQUE SHOPPING ARCADES

THE ROWS, CHESTER

Access

Most examples are on Eastgate Street and Bridge Street.

The 'Rows', or multi-storied covered medieval shopping arcades, are unique to Chester. The Rows consist of a double tier of shops, both levels being provided with footways, the upper one being set back and covered by the second storey of the buildings. In front of the first-floor footway is a continuous line of balconies.

They were built between the thirteenth and eighteenth centuries, and received their first mention in 1331. Whether they were a natural development or an act of deliberate town planning after the disastrous fire of 1278 that destroyed most of the city centre, is not known.

One theory is that the Rows are due to the massive presence of Roman buildings along the main streets, which may have led the shop builders in medieval times to build in front of them and at a higher level. It is certainly the case that the Rows only extend within the old Roman settlement of Chester.

In medieval times it was common for the town's trades to be gathered together, thus Eastgate was 'Cook's Row' and Northgate was 'Ironmonger's Row'. Bridge Street was 'Mercer's Row' and the Butter Stoups and Milk Stoups were at the junction of Eastgate and Northgate. There was also a 'Broken Shin Row'!

What is certain is that they have helped Chester retain its compact city centre to the present day.

ONE OF THE UK'S OLDEST RACECOURSES

THE RHOODEE, CHESTER

Chester's racecourse is one of the oldest in the country. The name 'Rhoodee' originates from 'Rood', another name for a cross, the base of which is said to still exist on the site, and 'eye', which described land partly surrounded by water. It is one of the most unusual and attractive racecourses in the UK.

In the Middle Ages, the area was used as a place of recreation. In the early sixteenth century, football matches between the shoemakers and the drapers began at the cross on the Rhoodee, but problems of violence (proving that this phenomenon is nothing new) led to the City Assembly banning it in 1540, to be replaced by foot races, and horse races.

Its position close to the river meant that it was not always in the pristine condition that it is today. In the nineteenth century, some racing writers described its course as either a 'soup plate' or a 'cockpit'. Its most famous race, the Chester Cup, started here in 1824 as the Tradesmen's Cup.

The course itself is 1 mile, 49 yards long, and is unique for the UK in that its size and layout make it possible for spectators to see the entire race without using binoculars. Most of the course is curving and there is only a short home straight.

Except on race days, there is free access to the site.

Access

Between the City Walls and the River Dee, via either Grosvenor Road (A483) or New Crane Street (A548).

A TOWER LOCATED ON A SPUR FROM THE MAIN CITY WALLS

WATER TOWER, CHESTER

This tower, forming part of the City Walls but located on the end of a spur from Bonewaldesthorne's Tower, was built to protect the city's harbours, which in the Middle Ages were close to this point. It is some 75ft high, and the River Dee would originally have flowed around it and under the arch of the spur wall. Its original name was New Tower.

It was built between 1322 and 1325, along with the spur wall, by John de Helpeston, at a cost of £100.

The usefulness of the Water Tower diminished over the years as the Dee gradually silted up. In 1730 the river was diverted to a new canalised course, which took it some distance to the west, and well away from the Water Tower. Today, the interior is open occasionally for exhibitions.

On another part of the walls, King Charles's Tower contains a small museum, opened at certain times. From this tower, in 1645, King Charles witnessed the closing stages of the defeat of his forces between Hoole Heath and the city, which had started at Rowton Moor. It is some 70ft high and has held the names Newton Tower and Phoenix Tower, after the emblem of the city's Painters, Glaziers, Embroiderers and Stationers Company, who used it as a meeting place in the seventeenth century.

Access

On the City Walls, on the north western corner of the city centre.

THE SMALLEST GATE IN CHESTER'S CITY WALLS

KALEYARD GATE

This is the smallest gateway in Chester's historic City Walls. Tradition says that in 1275, the monks of St Werbergh's Abbey (now the Cathedral) were allowed to make this gateway to give them access to their vegetable gardens, or kaleyards, just outside the walls. The condition for this permission was that the gateway was locked at dusk every night, when the 'curfew bell' rang, a rule that was still observed by the Deans and Canons of the Cathedral until a few years ago. Nowadays, it is only closed occasionally in order to preserve its private status.

Round the other side of the Cathedral is the modern bell tower, called the Dean Addleshaw Tower, said to be the first free-standing cathedral bell tower to be built for an English cathedral since the fifteenth century. It is a concrete structure, infilled with brick and clad in slates.

Access

Either from Frodsham Street, or from Northgate, through the Abbey Gateway, the attractive Abbey Square and along Abbey Sreet. The gateway is down the narrow path to the right at the end of the street.

THIS ROOM USED TO BE WITHIN ANOTHER BUILDING

KING'S ARMS KITCHEN, GROSVENOR MUSEUM

This dark and panelled room came from a public house called the King's Arms Kitchen, which stood at the rear of a building which backed onto Eastgate. Access was gained by means of a narrow passageway next to the City Walls. The room was transferred to the museum in 1979 when the pub ceased to exist.

The room was in fact the 'Mayoral Parlour' of the 'Honourable Incorporation of the King's Arms Kitchen', and was the meeting place of a gentlemen's club. The club itself was formed in 1770, and formed a mock corporation, with its own Aldermen, Mayor, Sheriff, Town Clerk and other high offices of local government. The story goes that it was set up after a dispute over whether the Mayor should be elected by the Aldermen or the Freemen of the City.

The club existed for men to drink and to place bets. Its activities were meticulously recorded in a minute book. Many prominent citizens of Chester were members, although clergymen were not favoured. After the last 'election' in 1897, membership declined through lack of interest.

The room is furnished from the early nineteenth century, but the boards around the wall bear the names of past Mayors and Town Clerks of the Honourable Incorporation of the late eighteenth century. The diamond-headed oak panels are thought have been made from the wood from the old box pews of St John's Church, when they were removed. Unsuspecting visitors were invited to sit in the Mayor's chair, only then to be told it was their obligation to buy a round of drinks! This ruse continued in the room long after the mock corporation had ended its existence.

THE BRIDGE WHERE THE CONDEMNED WERE LED ACROSS

THE BRIDGE OF SIGHS, NORTHGATE

This little sandstone bridge, disused for many years and now without its iron railings, linked the Bluecoat School, created in 1717 by Bishop Stratford to house and educate poor boys, with the city's former gaol, which was located in the city's old Northgate. Prisoners were kept in dungeons cut deep in the sandstone below the City Wall, their cells having no windows.

The southern wing of the school housed the chapel of Little St John, where condemned criminals were taken, via the little bridge, to receive their last rites before execution.

The bridge itself was built in 1793, as a means of stopping the frequent attempts made to rescue inmates being led through the streets to the chapel.

Access

Visible from the western side of Northgate, where the road crosses the Shropshire Union Canal.

A CHURCH WITH A THREE-DECKER PULPIT

ST MICHAEL'S CHURCH, SHOTWICK

Shotwick is a little village that is literally now at the end of the road, and is very much a backwater. However, in the Middle Ages it was on a main salt route into Wales, which is only a mile away, crossing the old route of the River Dee by way of a ford. Henry III passed through with an army in 1245, as did Edward 'Longshanks' I in 1278 and 1284. The bowmen of Shotwick became renowned for their skills, the church porch showing arrow grooves arising from the obligation of all able-bodied men to practice archery on Sunday after Mass.

Access

Via Shotwick Lane, which runs westwards from Welsh Road (A550).

A church existed on this site in Saxon times, and the earliest parts of the current building are Norman. The church was rebuilt and extended in the fourteenth century. A tower was added in the fifteenth century.

Inside the church can be seen a churchwarden's pew, dating from 1673, a time when only the wardens had a seat provided for them. When box pews were installed in 1710, a canopy was put over the seat to distinguish it from the rest.

The triple-decker pulpit was bought second-hand in 1812. The clerk occupied the lowest deck, with the minister running the service from the middle deck and preaching from the top.

In the seventeenth century, the village acquired a reputation as the English 'Gretna Green' in view of the large number of marriages conducted at the former Greyhound Inn, now Greyhound Farm, almost opposite the church. These irregular marriages were conducted by the curate, or by the local schoolmaster, and efforts by the Church authorities to exert some form of control over this activity were not totally effective.

A WINDMILL NAMED AFTER A PUNISHMENT FOR MURDER

GIBBET MILL, SAUGHALL

This mill is named after an event that took place in August 1750, when three Irish labourers robbed and murdered a traveller (some say a fourth labourer) after getting inebriated at the former Greyhound Inn, now Greyhound Farm, at Shotwick. They were observed in this deed by a farm labourer and were caught at Shotwick, kept overnight in a barn and taken to Chester Castle the following day.

They were duly tried, but one of the men turned 'King's Evidence', helping to convict the other two, who were found guilty on 8 September. They were hanged at Broughton on 22 September. Their bodies were 'hung up in irons near the Two Mills on the Heath, in the road to Parkgate', at or near the current location of Gibbet Mill.

The current mill was built shortly before 1773, and was working until 1926. It became a private house in 1960.

Access

On the eastern side of the A540, just north of its junction with the A5117 and M56.

MARKING THE CENTRE OF THE WIRRAL 'HUNDRED'

THE WIRRAL STONE, WILLASTON

Access

At the junction of Chester High Road (A540) and Hadlow Road (B5151).

This stone, known as the 'Wirral Stone', is a bit of a mystery. Theories as to its origin range from it being some form of Roman marker used in surveying the Cheshire area, that it marks the centre of the old Wirral 'Hundred' (an old local government land division) where the Hundred Court actually met, or that it was some form of mounting stone, an idea supported by its stepped shape.

It is also said to be the inspiration for the naming of Willaston itself, though claims are made that the true 'Wirhealstone' lies buried in the centre of the village, under the road close to the Old Red Lion Inn. In the earlier years of the twentieth century, older residents could recall a large round stone about 3 ft across, around which children used to play 'Jack Stones'.

The Wirral Stone was restored in 1993.

ONLY THE TRAINS ARE MISSING AT THIS 1950s STATION

HADLOW ROAD STATION, WILLASTON

This former railway station, now part of the Wirral Way Country Park, has been recreated to look exactly as it would have done in 1952, complete with porter's trolley, milk churns, enamel advertising signs, luggage and ticket office furniture. A short stretch of track has been re-laid, but alas there are no trains calling!

The station was on the line that was opened from Hooton to Parkgate in October 1861, being extended to West Kirby in 1866. Unfortunately, it was only a single track with passing loops so the service would never have been very frequent. It closed to passengers in 1956 and to goods in 1962.

In 1969 it was bought, along with the rest of the line's trackbed, by Cheshire County Council, to form the Wirral Way Country Park, which opened in 1973 and was one of the first such parks in the UK. The signal box and level crossing gates are not original to the site however: they were moved here from Hassall Green, near Crewe.

Access

On the B5151 (Hadlow Road) about 400 yards south of the centre of Willaston.

A FINE EXAMPLE OF A TOWER MILL

WILLASTON WINDMILL

Access

To the south of Mill Lane, on the northern edges of the village.

This windmill was built in 1800 on the same site as several earlier mills. It was one of the largest tower mills to be built in the Wirral, and remained in use up to 1930, when its sails were destroyed in a storm.

One of its millers earned a reputation for being one of the most well organised in the country. Within the space of one day, he is said to have had the corn cut and threshed, ground and turned into bread, and then made sure it was delivered to London by the evening.

The mill no longer possesses its sails and is now a private house.

A PLACE FOR STRAY ANIMALS OR DEBTORS' CATTLE

THE PINFOLD, CAPENHURST

This sandstone enclosure, about 6 yards square, is an old animal pound or 'pinfold' (alternative 'penfold'), and dates from the tenth century. Pinfolds were looked after by a 'pound-keeper' and were used for holding stray animals, where they were kept until reclaimed by the owner, who had to pay for any damage caused by the strays. The owners had a 'right of rescue' if they saw their animals in the process of being taken to the pinfold.

They were also used for holding domestic animals or cattle. In past times, it was possible for creditors to seize the animals of anyone who owed them debts. They would be taken to the pound and kept there, at the debtor's expense, until the debt was paid.

A stone on the site records its restoration by the local parish council with help from Chester City Council. Other pinfolds are to be found at Little Budworth and at Spital.

The nearby church, Holy Trinity, built in 1856-9, has an unusual pagoda-like wooden tower and matching lych-gate.

Access

On the south side of Capenhurst Lane, close to the church.

REMINDERS OF THE DAYS WHEN QUAKERISM WAS REGARDED AS EVIL

QUAKER GRAVES, BURTON

Access

On the edge of Burton Wood, at the side of a footpath close to Burton church.

These two gravestone slabs are enclosed by iron railings. They date from the time when Quakers were regarded by the established Church as 'an active spirit of evil', bringing 'contamination and disgrace in everything connected with it.'

The inscriptions on the two slabs are worn away, due to the fact that the stones were originally in the centre of the pathway, but they were recorded in 1870, when still partly visible. A date of 1663 was found on one of them.

Although locally known as the 'Quaker Graves', it is not certain that they are of Quakers. There is no evidence of Quakerism in the area during this period, which was at a time when the movement was first establishing itself.

The graves are thought to be those of a man and his wife, who, for some reason, could not be buried in consecrated ground.

A local sign records that they have been preserved 'as a tribute to the men and women who adopted a courageous attitude in difficult times.'

A CHURCH CLOCK WITH ONLY ONE HAND

CHURCH CLOCK, BURTON

The attractive church of St Nicholas, built in 1721, is the third church on this site, the earliest of which dated from the eleventh century.

    The church itself contains many interesting features, including a Jacobean communion rail, thought to be the oldest in the Wirral, and the three money bags carved on the lectern. St Nicholas is said to be the patron saint of pawnbrokers, supposedly after he donated three bags of gold to a poor family who could not afford to pay for their daughters' weddings.

    On one of the walls is a lozenge-shaped board known as a 'hatchment', containing the coats of arms of the Congreve and Birch families. When a person of local standing dies, it was common to set up such a board above their front door for a year and a day, after which it was placed in the local church as a memorial. This one is thought to be for Richard Congreve, who died in 1857.

    Outside, on the tower, can be seen this one-handed clock, one of a small number of such 'Turret Clocks' built by Joseph Smith in 1751. In those days, it was only necessary to know the hour, and as clocks were so inaccurate, minute hands were useless. Stoak church, to the north east of Chester, also has a single hand and is also by Joseph Smith.

Access

In the centre of the village, via The Rake.

A WELL DATING FROM THE IRON AGE

HAMPSTON'S WELL, BURTON

Access

Located on
the southern
side of Station
Road to the
west of the
village.

According to the information board on the site, this well, or rather spring, served the Iron Age settlements at Burton Point, and the Anglo-Saxon settlement of Burton, from about AD 900.

The earliest known written records are from 1602/3, when it was referred to as Patrick's Well. There are frequent references in the records of the local Manor Court to its upkeep, as it was important in the days before piped water to ensure the purity of supply from such sources of water.

The local constables were required to clean the well every year and all the local able-bodied men were obliged to help or else face a fine of 6 (old) pence, equivalent in those days to a couple of days' wages. The Manor Court also passed bylaws to raise funds for its maintenance from the locals, to prohibit the washing of clothes at the well, and to prevent anyone from diverting the well water from its usual course.

It had become known as Hampston's Well by the nineteenth century, and was named after a family who had lived in the village since the sixteenth century.

After lying neglected and forgotten for a number of years, the well and surroundings were restored by Ellesmere Port and Neston Borough Council in 1975 in honour of Councillor Horace Green, who had served on Neston Urban District Council for twenty-six years, and who died in 1973.

ONCE A BUSY PORT FOR IRELAND

PARKGATE

Parkgate is an attractive village on the western side of the Wirral peninsula, with views out across the Dee towards North Wales. It is an attractive spot and a popular tourist location. Its name came from the nearby Neston Park, and the village developed after the estate was sold in 1599.

Today, although there is a promenade, the sea is quite far out and the foreshore is mostly grass and salt marsh. Between 1686 and 1815, it was both a bathing establishment and a sea port. In fact, it was one of the principal departure points for Ireland before Thomas Telford built the road through North Wales now known as the A5, which allowed quicker access to the Emerald Isle via Holyhead.

John Wesley crossed from here to Ireland. So, reputedly, (in 1741) did George Frederick Handel, on his way to Dublin and the first performance of his famous 'Messiah', although it is known that in fact, after waiting several fruitless days at Parkgate, he went on to Holyhead. He did, however, return via Parkgate.

Because use of the port was dependent on the tides, boats had to be loaded off-shore. Assembly rooms were built for entertaining the waiting passengers, as well as baths and gambling establishments. For a time Parkgate attracted a smart and fashionable clientele.

In the first part of the nineteenth century, Parkgate began to decline. Its role as a port ended when Telford finished his road and the Dee was artificially forced to flow along the Welsh shore. The development of New Brighton took away the tourists.

The locally-made ice creams are to be recommended.

Access

The B5134 leads along the 'seafront' at Parkgate.

NOT A MEMORIAL TO ADMIRAL NELSON AT ALL

'NELSON' STONES, PARKGATE

Access

On Station Road, close to the 'seafront'.

On the corner of The Parade and Station Road stands Dover Cottage, an eighteenth-century building where Emma Lyon came to stay in June 1784 to cure herself of a skin complaint. Emma, originally called Amy, had been born in the village, and was later to become Lady Hamilton and Lord Nelson's mistress.

Next door, spelled out in the cobbles in front of another cottage, is the name 'Nelson'. This does not, as is frequently thought, commemorate the famous Admiral, but Nelson Burt, the son of a noted Chester artist, Albin Burt, who painted miniature portraits. After young Nelson's death in 1822 from drowning, his father commemorated his son by setting out the stones we see today.

A CHURCH CONNECTED WITH A ONE-TIME ARCHBISHOP

PLEMSTALL CHURCH

This is one of those Cheshire churches that stands isolated at the end of a rural cul-de-sac. The surrounding land is mainly low-lying and was frequently flooded. The church is dedicated to St Peter.

In the latter half of the ninth century, a Mercian cleric called Plegmund lived here as a hermit. He became well known in the area for his learning and spiritual life, and when Alfred the Great ascended the throne of England, he called Plegmund to his court to help him with various literary works. His assistance was mentioned in the preface to Alfred's version of Pope Gregory's '*Regula Pastoralis*', and it is also asserted that he worked on part of the Winchester Codex of the Anglo-Saxon Chronicle.

By 890 Plegmund had been made Archbishop of Canterbury, and it was therefore his duty to crown Alfred's son, Edward, in 901. He visited the Pope twice during his reign as Archbishop and after his death in 914, he was buried in Canterbury Cathedral.

A couple of minutes' walk further back along the lane is Plegmund's Well, which is traditionally belived to be where he used to baptise his new believers. It was restored early in the twentieth century, and was provided with a decorative archway in 2002.

Outside the church, at the eastern end, is a curious tomb with two skeletons, one male and one female, carved on the long sides. This is the tombchest and memorial to the Hurleston family, and dates from 1670. It is reputedly the site of Plegmund's hermitage.

Access

Via Plemstall Lane, which is off the eastern side of the A56 in Mickle Trafford.

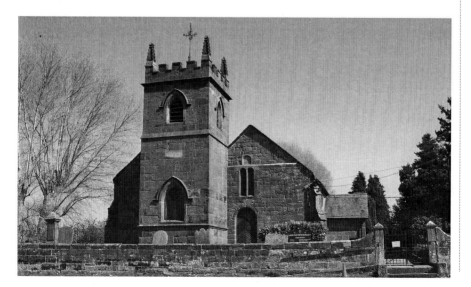

A HOUSE THAT HAS BEEN MOVED MANY MILES

AUSTERSON OLD HALL, ALVANLEY

This building, located on one side of Alvanley Hill, is a timber-framed building, most likely dating from the sixteenth or seventeenth centuries. It is 'listed' as being of architectural or historic importance and has a Grade II star classification.

It was originally located at Old Hall Farm, Coole Lane, Austerson, near Hack Green, south of Nantwich, but was rebuilt here between 1974 and 1986 by James Brotherhood – an architect specialising in the conservation of historic buildings – from his workshop on the site. The Hall was re-erected by local craftsmen, using oak and elm from the firm of Henry Venables in Stafford and glass and leadwork from Victoria Glass in the Wirral.

The Hall is a fine example of a Cheshire timber-framed house, originally built for a yeoman of some social standing. The reconstruction has been undertaken sympathetically, re-using old materials when possible. It was re-listed by English Heritage on its re-erection because of the quality of the restoration and its historical detailing.

Relocating timber-framed buildings has been undertaken on a number of occasions, with the timber frame being easily re-erected on the new site, and the walls and roof following. Three seventeenth-century timber-framed buildings from the site of Manchester Airport's second runway were relocated and re-erected between 1998 and 2009, in North Cheshire, the architect on each occasion being James Brotherhood.

AN ATTRACTIVE VILLAGE WELL

DENE WELL HOUSE, GREAT BUDWORTH

This pleasant little well house near the attractive village of Great Budworth was built in 1880 and was paid for by the Egerton Warburtons of Arley Hall. The building was designed by the church architect, Edmund Kirby. The verse above the well spout was the work of the 'rhyming squire of Arley', Rowland Egerton-Warburton (*see* page 74).

The well was regularly used by the village until 1934, when piped water arrived. Some time before this, the earth slope above the well was investigated as the well water had acquired a distinctive taste. The cause of the problem was found to be contamination of the water by a dead donkey!

The water is said to be fit to drink today, but the authorities give no assuarance that this will always be the case!

Access

At the junction of Northwich Road (A559) with High Street, which leads up to the village.

A CHEST THAT CAN ONLY BE OPENED BY FIVE SEPARATE KEYS

ST MARY AND ALL SAINTS' CHURCH, GREAT BUDWORTH

Access

The church is situated in the centre of the village.

St Mary and All Saints' Church in Great Budworth is rated by the writer Simon Jenkins as one of the thousand most beautiful churches in England

Inside, on both sides of the entrance to the Warburton Chapel, are two chests. The one on the right dates from the Middle Ages, and is made from thick oak planks held together with wide wrought-iron bands made by the local blacksmith. The chest has five separate locks, the keys of which were held separately by the priest and the churchwardens. It held the church's valuable plate, vestments, service books and Bibles, and could only be opened by all five keyholders together. A similar chest, carved from a hollowed-out tree, and dating from 1269, can be found in St Oswald's Church at Lower Peover.

The other chest is dated 1680, and has front panels carved with flowers and bunches of grapes. Towards the rear of the church on the wall a table of parish fees dating from 1863.

Outside in the churchyard is the former school, dating from 1600, and built with money donated by John Dean of London. It looks typical of the houses in the rest of the village. It ceased to be used as the village's school in 1857, when it was replaced by a building nearby.

A short distance beyond the churchyard is the delightful avenue of yew trees, which form a pleasant tree-lined path.

THE LAST OPEN PAN SALT WORKS IN CHESHIRE

LION SALT WORKS, MARSTON

Access

On the eastern side of Ollershaw Lane (B5075) about half a mile north of Northwich, just before the canal bridge.

Since Roman times, salt has been produced in Cheshire by the open pan method of evaporation. Natural brine is the result of ground water reaching rock salt and forming underground brine streams. The brine is about eight times saltier than sea water.

In 1842, the Thompson family moved to Marston and set up a salt works at the Adelaide Mine to produce fishery salt, bay salt, crystal and lump salt. By the end of the nineteenth century, two brothers, John William and Henry Ingram Thompson, were operating separate works at the current location. Eventually, after many disputes with his brother, Henry bought him out and the company traded under the name Henry Ingram Thompson & Sons.

The works were constantly being enlarged and rebuilt, and recurring subsidence meant that the buildings were usually fairly flimsy structures. In 1900, there were three pans and a stove for making fine salt, and four pans for common salt. A pan house was added as late as the 1960s. Both canal and railway were used to transport the finished products to market or port for export.

The company was still trading in the early 1980s, making lump salt for health food shops and for the Nigerian market. Visitors were shown round the site at weekends by former employees. The works however closed for good in 1986, when the export market collapsed.

Since then, the site has been bought by the local authority, and, through the work of a charitable trust, it is slowly being brought back into a suitable condition for access by visitors.

ONE OF THE WONDERS OF THE WATERWAYS

ANDERTON BOAT LIFT

Access

The main car park (well signposted) is off New Road, which leads eastwards off the A533 about half a mile north of Northwich.

The Trent & Mersey Canal, which connects the North West with the Midlands and the South, passes close to the Weaver Navigation, which linked the Cheshire saltfield with the Mersey estuary at Anderton. Unfortunately, the level of the canal is some 50ft above that of the river, and it was never considered viable to construct an expensive series of locks to connect the two. As a result, such transhipment that did take place was by means of manual chutes.

In 1875, Edward Leader Williams, engineer to the Weaver Navigation Trustees (and later to be the designer of the Manchester Ship Canal) designed the boat lift to solve the transhipment problem. Although small boat lifts had been tried before on the tub boat canals of Devon and Cornwall, they had never worked properly and had all been abandoned after a few years of operation. The Anderton Lift, however, would have none of these problems. It was hydraulically operated and could raise or lower a barge or a pair of narrow boats in just five minutes. Between 1906 and 1908, its design was altered and it was converted to run on electricity, which meant that each caisson could now be operated independently. In the 1970s it was still carrying pleasure craft.

Deterioration of its ironwork caused it to be closed to traffic in 1983, but it was restored in 2000-2 at a cost of £7 million. It now runs again on hydraulic operation, although the 'A' frames and pulleys installed in the 1907 conversion were left in place for historical purposes.

Boat trips up and down the lift are available on 'high days and holidays', and there is an interesting visitor centre.

NORTHWICH'S FLOATING BRIDGES

TOWN BRIDGE AND HAYHURST BRIDGE, NORTHWICH

Northwich is a town built on salt. Whether salt has been removed by mining or by brine extraction methods, the town in past years has been badly affected by subsidence.

When the Town Bridge and its upstream colleague, Hayhurst Bridge, were built by the Trustees of the Weaver Navigation in 1899, the bridges had to be made to withstand the effects of any likely subsidence. They also had to be swing bridges to allow barges and small sea-going vessels to be able to navigate the river as far as Winsford.

J.E. Saner, chief engineer to the Trustees, came up with an ingenious solution to the problem; three-fifths of the bridges' weight is taken by a floating pontoon, which moves with the bridge. Eight steel piles around the pontoon take the rest of the weight. The piles themselves support a roller channel which allow the bridge to swing. This can be adjusted in height to counteract any subsidence and keep the bridge level.

The bridges have been operated by electricity from the outset and are believed to be the world's oldest electric swing bridges. They were strengthened to take heavier loads in 1998.

Access

On the western side of the town centre.

THE SLOWEST MOBILE LIBRARY IN THE COUNTRY

BRUNNER LIBRARY, NORTHWICH

Access

On the northern side of Witton Street, in the town centre.

Northwich's town centre buildings have shown an amazing ability to disappear over the years, as vast holes in the ground appeared as a result of salt mining and brine extraction. One three-storey building in 1920 is reported to have fallen backwards into a hole that had appeared, finishing up at an angle of 45 degrees.

Consequently, many of Northwich's buildings are timber-framed, enabling them to withstand changes in ground level, and to be re-positioned to the upright. Northwich's main street is comprised of many such structures and is more modern than its appearance belies.

Northwich's attractive Brunner Library, donated to the town by Sir John Brunner and situated on the main street, is a case in point. It was first built as a library and salt museum in 1886 by two local salt proprietors, Thomas Ward and John Brunner, who felt that the town needed something to explain its status as the 'salt capital of the world'. The building was donated to the town in 1889, only for it to collapse as a result of subsidence some twenty years later.

The current building, designed by A.E. Bowles, was provided in 1909, also paid for by Sir John Brunner, as a replacement, being opened by the Rt Hon. W. Runeiman MP. It contained a newsroom, magazine room, reference library, lending library, ladies room and museum. It is still the town's main library and is now a Grade II listed building.

Subsidence is still affecting the building, and it is reputed to move half an inch a year, making it the 'slowest mobile library in the country'.

PART OF NORTHWICH'S INDUSTRIAL HISTORY

EDWARDIAN PUMPING STATION, NORTHWICH

This elegant little circular brick building was opened in 1913. It was used to pump sewage from the lower parts of Northwich 'uphill' to the treatment works at Wallerscote. Before it was built, untreated sewage discharged directly into the river and caused pollution.

The pumping was done by gas engines, and these are demonstrated today, although they now only pump water. The station remained in use for over sixty years, until the pumps were superseded by electric ones. The pumping station, now a Grade II listed building, opened to the public in 1993.

Nearby is Northwich's Salt Museum, which is well worth a visit.

Access

At the end of Weir Street, which is on the western side of London Road (A533), just south of the town centre. The pumping station is open on weekend afternoons between Easter and the end of September.

ONCE AN ENTRANCE TO A COUNTRY ESTATE

ROUND TOWER LODGE, SANDIWAY

This little building, variously called the Round Tower Lodge, Round Lodge or Tower Lodge, is situated in the middle of the A556 dual carriageway. Demolition was threatened when the road was being 'dualled' in the 1930s, but fortunately the new (westbound) carriageway was constructed to the south of the tower.

It is not known precisely when the tower was built, but it is thought to be from the early nineteenth century. It was originally part of one of the gate lodges to the New Park of Vale Royal Abbey. Constructed of sandstone, it is a two-storey building, surmounted by a castellated parapet. There are glazed windows on the ground floor and unglazed crossloops on the first floor. On the eastern side is a short stub wall which led to a single-storey extension, no longer remaining. Further extensions were made to this room in the late nineteenth and early twentieth centuries.

In 1871, the lodge was being lived in by a shepherd, William Ree, and his family. Hughie Preston and his wife were the last tenants in the 1920s. New Park became Pettypool Park in the late nineteenth century and became the base of Sandiway Golf Club after 1918.

King Charles is reputed to have hidden in the tower whilst escaping, and it is reputedly protected by Royal Charter, but this is a myth as the tower was not even built at that time.

It is currently a Grade II listed building and is owned by the Highways Agency, who carried out some restoration in 2002.

Access

On the A556, just west of its junction with the A559.

A PUB NAMED AFTER A FAMOUS CHESHIRE HOUND

BLUE CAP HOTEL, SANDIWAY

This public house on the main road commemorates 'Blue Cap', a famous Cheshire black-pied foxhound from the eighteenth century.

The traditional meeting point of the Cheshire Hunt was at the pub, opposite the Hunt's kennels. Local children were given the day off school to watch the event, and carriages – and later cars – would follow the hounds.

It is said that all Cheshire Hounds are descended from Blue Cap. In 1763, when he was four, his master, the Hon. John Smith-Barry of Marbury Hall, issued a challenge to the Master of the Quorn Hunt (from Leicestershire), Hugo Meynell. Any two Quorn hounds would race against Blue Cap and Wanton, his daughter. The money at stake between the two challengers was 500 guineas, with separate wagers between their respective supporters.

The race took place at Newmarket Heath on 30 September over a course of 4 miles. Blue Cap and Wanton came first and second respectively, despite Blue Cap being given a weighted collar to keep him at the same speed as the rest of the field. The Quorn's bitch refused to race at all. The local pub, until then known as the Sandiway Head, was then renamed the Blue Cap Hotel, which it retains to this day.

Blue Cap lived another nine years. He was buried in the pub's garden, but was moved to the kennels by the Cheshire Hunt in the 1950s in a bid to deter visitors to the pub who didn't buy a drink.

Access

On the northern side of Chester Road (A556), about half a mile east of its junction with the A49.

WHERE THE SALTERS ALLOWED THEIR HORSES TO TAKE WATER

SALTERS WELL, TARPORLEY

Access

On Salter Well
Lane, which
leads into
Tarporley from
the A49/A51
roundabout.

The pleasant town of Tarporley was located on the 'Salter's Route', by which salt from Northwich, Middlewich and Nantwich was taken to markets in Chester and North Wales up to the end of the eighteenth century. The attractive Salter's Well on the outskirts of the town was where the salters allowed their horses to take water.

Now unfortunately dry, this attractive well was restored by the local authority in 1983, assisted by a donation from the owner of the adjoining Salterswell House.

Elsewhere in the town, the old fire station, now a fire service museum, is well worth a visit. Started as an independent voluntary fire service by the Earl of Harrington in 1866, the museum building served as the fire station until 1957, when it was relocated to what is now the chocolate shop on the High Street. This remained in use until 1993, when a purpose-built station was provided on Birch Heath Road.

Next door to the post office is a rare example of a traditional 'K6' telephone box, designed by Sir Giles Gilbert Scott in 1935. It is listed as being of architectural and historical importance.

On the eastern side of the High Street, a stone plaque commemorates four almshouses dating from 1704, which stood on an adjacent site until 1962.

A VERY DISTINCTIVE CURIOSITY

ELEPHANT AND CASTLE, PECKFORTON

This is a true curiosity and a piece of whimsy. Carved from a lovely red sandstone and finished around 1859, it is the work of a local stonemason, John (or William) Watson. It is made out of a single block of stone from the same quarry at Firbank as that used for stone for Peckforton Castle. Watson was at the time working on the castle, having earlier being foreman mason for the building of Chester's Grosvenor Bridge.

The structure adorned his own cottage garden, called appropriately 'Elephant and Castle Cottage'. The elephant has a tasselled saddle, which supports the three-tiered castle, compete with turreted gatehouse and a keep with turrets at the corners. The animal's tusks have subsequently been broken. Some of the windows contain glass, and it is suggested that it was originally intended to be a beehive. Certainly, at the time of this author's visit, it appeared to be popular with the bees.

The elephant is approximately two-thirds life size and was commissioned in the early 1850s by Edwin Corbet, then living at Tilstone Lodge. It never made it there as Corbet died in 1858 before it was finished. Carved on it is the inscription 'Sacred to the memory of Edwin Corbet', together with the family crest.

An elephant was part of the coat of arms of the Corbett family, who owned Peckforton before 1626. The 'elephant and castle' is also a common public house name, but Peckforton has never had a pub of that name. It is also part of the crest of the Worshipful Company of Cutlers.

Access

Off Quarry Bank, which leads westwards off Stone House Lane.

THE UK'S LARGEST AND OLDEST COMMERCIAL SALT MINE

WINSFORD SALT MINE

This is the UK's largest commercial salt mine, one of only three such places in the country, the others being in North Yorkshire and Northern Ireland.

Rock salt was laid down in Cheshire over 220 million years ago. Sea water moved inland, creating a series of shallow salt marshes. As the sea retreated and the marshes evaporated, thick deposits of rock salt became part of the local geology.

Salt extraction began in the seventeenth century, and the current mine, originally known as Meadow Bank Mine, dates from 1844. Mining is from a depth of 150 to 190 metres and is undertaken by the 'room and pillar' method of mining. The average roof height of 8 metres and width of 20 metres makes this a relatively safe working environment when compared to coal mining.

One of the Caterpillar diggers working underground is understood to be the largest in the world. Its tyres are 9.5 ft high.

The mine produces about one million tons a year and has a network of 135 miles of tunnels spread over several square miles, stretching from Winsford to Northwich.

The dimensions and conditions of the mine make it ideal for record storage, and in recent years, worked-out parts of the mine have been used to store confidential government files, hospital records, material belonging to the National Archives and business data.

Access

To the north of the town, via New Road and Bradford Road.

A COMBINED VILLAGE CROSS AND LOCK-UP

OVER CROSS, WINSFORD

This village cross, built in the form of a stepped pyramid with a cross on the top, is unusual in that it also forms the village lock-up.

Built in 1830, and therefore a late example of a lock-up, the Cross was used to detain drunks, thieves and swindlers who plagued the nearby Over Market. The wrongdoers were held overnight and then sentenced by the Mayor at the magistrates' court when it was in session at the George and Dragon public house. More serious offenders would be sent on to the Chester Assize Courts or the magistrates' court at Oakmere.

It is believed that the cross was constructed around an earlier lock-up. Its use as a lock-up would have been short-lived after police stations – with their own cells – began to be constructed in the latter part of the nineteenth century. The lock-up, to which access was gained via the rear (currently in the school grounds), was used as a coal store for the school's boilers until the 1960s, but the doorway was blocked up in the 1970s.

There are some curious tales of secret passages and buried treasure associated with the cross, although none of these have any truth. The nearby street called Saxon Crossway was invented by the local authority in the 1960s when the adjoining estate was constructed; it commemorates the real Saxon cross, a fragment of which is preserved in St Chad's Church.

Access

On the eastern side of Delamere Street, which leads northwards from the A54, adjacent to St John's Primary School.

DOES THIS TREE REALLY MARK THE CENTRE OF CHESHIRE?

COMMEMORATIVE OAK, BOSTOCK GREEN

The two plaques at the base of this large oak tree record that this tree was planted in the centre of Cheshire by three individuals, namely the Revd Canon, Colonel and Captain Hayhurst in 1887, the jubilee year of Queen Victoria.

The Revd Canon Thomas France Hayhursts (1839-1889) was the brother of Colonel Charles Hosken Hayhurst (1832-1914), and Captain William Hosken France-Hayhurst (who died in 1929) was the rector's son.

Access

On the eastern side of the unclassified road that runs through the village, opposite the junction with Brick Kiln Lane.

The family lived at Bostock Hall from 1775, until the Hall was sold to Manchester Corporation in 1955 for use as a school. The family was responsible for many developments in the area, including the redevelopment of the village between 1850 and 1875.

Precisely how the tree's location as the 'centre of Cheshire' claim could be made is not known, and it would certainly refer to the pre-1974 boundaries, along which the northern boundaries of the county are considerably different from today's administrative county.

This tree was planted during the 1887 Jubilee celebrations on the site of an earlier 'ancient oak', which had become unsafe and potentially dangerous by the early 1880s.

IT LOOKS LIKE A DOVECOTE, BUT IS SOMETHING RATHER DIFFERENT!

THE WINNING POST, CHRISTLETON

This mysterious hexagonal structure, which resembles a small dovecote, complete with pyramidical roof, was built in 1900 by Adams of York as part of the local authority sewage system. Officially it was known as 'Christleton Sewage Lift'.

It was built when the local area was being provided with a sewerage system. Because of a rise in the ground level between the village and Chester, the area's sewage, if allowed to flow naturally, would have emptied into the Caldy Brook. This, in turn, discharged into the River Dee, near the main inlet pipes of the Chester Waterworks. Alarmed at the prospect of their supply being contaminated, Chester Waterworks obliged the local township to come to an agreement, whereby the latter provided the sewage lift if the former supplied pressured water.

Access

On the western side of Whitchurch Road (A41).

The sewage was collected in a ground-level tank. When it reached a certain level, water was released from the header tank in the tower allowing the sewage to be flushed over the rise in the ground, thus allowing it to flow into the City of Chester's main sewage system. The mechanism was, reputedly, not always reliable!

It has not been used for this purpose since the end of the Second World War, when it was replaced by an electric pumping station. However its place as a local landmark is assured and it is kept in good condition.

The name 'Winning Post' arose from the pre-motorway era, when local motorists travelling from the south towards Chester along the A41 realised that they were nearly 'home' and had almost reached the city's boundaries.

COMMEMORATING A MAN WHO KEPT A ZOO IN HIS BASEMENT

WILLIAM HUGGINS' GRAVE, ST JAMES'S CHURCH, CHRISTLETON

Access

St James's Church is located in the centre of the village of Christleton, at the junction of Pepper Street and Little Heath Road. The gravestone is to the right of the main path leading to the church's entrance.

This gravestone, made from pink sandstone, commemorates William and Samuel Huggins, an accomplished painter and architect respectively. William was born in Liverpool in 1820, and as early as the age of 15 he was demonstrating his ability as a painter when he was awarded a prize by the Mechanics' Institute for a historical painting.

The brothers came to live at Rock House, Christleton in 1878, on the death of William's wife. William made himself a name as a fine painter of animals (especially the big cats), portraits and the Cheshire countryside. His paintings were exhibited at the Royal Academy at various times between 1846 and 1875. He died in February 1884. It is thought that he was responsible for his own epitaphs on the gravestone, which are: 'an Historic and Animal Painter of acknowledged eminence' and 'A just and compassionate man who would neither tread on a worm nor cringe to an emperor'.

It is rumoured that he kept a small zoo of animals in the basement of Rock House (currently a dentist's surgery), so that he could paint them more accurately from life.

Close by, at the base of the church tower, is a small boundary stone. This has the date 1847 and the initials 'CP LT' carved on it, which stand for 'Christleton Parish/ Littleton Township'. It was rescued in the 1960s by some of the church's bell ringing team from being destroyed by road improvements at its previous site near the Vicar's Cross roundabout.

A FORTIFIED WATER TOWER

WATER TOWER, SAIGHTON

This is a remarkably war-like castellated structure, built in red sandstone. Due to its location in the local landscape, it looks taller from a distance than it actually is: close up it is more modest in scale. It dates from about 1870, and is simply a water tower.

It owes its ornate castellated appearance to the insistence of Countess Grosvenor, and was probably designed to reflect the former Saighton Grange, a very ornate house, of which little remains except the fifteenth-century gatehouse to the current-day Abbey Gate College.

Access

On the eastern side of Chapel Lane, near the centre of Saighton village.

THE HOME OF THE GROSVENOR FAMILY SINCE THE FIFTEENTH CENTURY

EATON HALL, EATON ESTATE

The Eaton estate extends to about 11,000 acres and is the country house to the Duke of Westminster, often said to be the wealthiest individual in the country. The estate has been in the family since the fifteenth century.

There have been at least four Eaton Halls. The first was built in brick by Sir John Vanbrugh at the end of the seventeenth century. William Porden reconstructed the Hall in a gothic style between 1804 and 1812. Further alterations and enhancements of the gothic style then took place in the 1870s when the Hall was massively expanded by Alfred Waterhouse at a cost of some £600,000, probably the most expensive project ever on an English country house, clearly reflecting the wealth of the family.

This version of Eaton Hall survived until the 1970s, having served as a military hospital in both the First and Second World Wars and as an officer cadet training school from 1946 to 1960. A large chapel, with bell tower, survives to this day; the tower was deliberately built to look like Big Ben and is sometimes called 'Little Ben'. At one time the song 'There's no place like home' was played on the bells each time the duke came home.

The Waterhouse Hall was largely demolished in the 1970s, and replaced by a large suburban style villa, which some claim resembled 'an Argentinian ranch house at the end of a dusty road'. In 1989, the external appearance of the Hall was substantially modified, and encased to give it a more classical appearance, which is the look it retains today. The present duke inherited the title and estate on the death of his father in 1979.

Access

Normal access to the estate is via the village of Eccleston and Paddock Road. Eaton Hall is not open to the public but the estate is opened on a few days each year.

THE SOLE REMINDER OF CHESHIRE'S COPPER MINING PAST

COPPER MINE CHIMNEY, GALLANTRY BANK

Access

On the
northern
side of the
A534, at its
junction with
Coppermines
Lane.

This isolated chimney – built in 1856 – is easily visible from the main road and is all that remains of the copper mining industry that was present among the Bickerton hills.

Gallantry Bank was originally called 'Gallows Tree Bank', and was named after the gibbeting there of a murderer named Holford in 1640.

Copper mining in Cheshire dates from about 1670, and a mine at this location was certainly being worked some twenty years later. The mining was never more than marginally viable, and was intermittent over the next two centuries. Various outside experts were asked for advice at various times. The year 1697 saw suggestions from a German, J.D. Brandshagen, whilst in 1806, Captain Thomas Dunstan (probably a mine captain rather than a seafarer) from Cornwall, offered his advice.

Mining last took place in the area in the 1920s, by which time it was very small scale, involving no more than three local men. Over the winter of 1928/9, the buildings were demolished and the shafts filled in or sealed, leaving just this isolated tower and the adjoining road name (Coppermines Lane) as the sole reminders of the industry.

WAS THIS THE HOME OF A MYSTERIOUS HERMIT?

MAD ALLEN'S HOLE, BICKERTON HILL

This difficult-to-find site is the reputed home of a late nineteenth-century hermit known as 'Mad Allen', who lived there for a time. Little is known about this individual and recent searches of the cave's interior have failed to find any evidence of human habitation.

The absence of information has led others to associate this cave with the so-called 'Allenscomb's Cave', the story of which was published by the Cheshire Archeological Society in 1864. In this, the story was told of a John Harris, born in 1710, who took to being a hermit after being refused permission by his parents to marry the love of his life. He then resolved never to marry as long as he lived, and 'have as little conversation with mankind as possible'.

Harris first lived in a cave in Carden Park (for which some evidence of habitation has been found), but after twenty years he moved to Allenscomb's cave, the location of which has not been discovered, but which is thought to be near Harthill and therefore some distance from Mad Allen's Hole. The whole tale is thought in certain quarters to be a myth.

Mad Allen's Hole is a natural two-level cave set in a low cliff face on the natural sandstone ridge at this point. Easy access to both levels can be gained via a hole at the back of the cave. A natural overhang is formed by the huge boulders at the cave's entrance, over which a timber front could easily have been built.

Access

This can be accessed via the Sandstone Trail. Approximately half a mile west of Goldford Lane, the trail passes a sandstone rock overhang carved with graffiti. To get access to Mad Allen's Hole, you need to descend about 15ft and climb along the hillside opposite at this point, working your way eastwards. Only do this if you are able and fit and prepared to accept a degree of personal risk, as the paths are ill-defined and the ground steep and treacherous.

A MAGNIFICENT PREHISTORIC EARTHWORK

MAIDEN CASTLE, BICKERTON

Access

Either via the
Sandstone
Trail, or park
in the small
National Trust
car park, which
is at the end of
an unnamed
road, which
leads off Old
Coach Road,
about 1.5
miles south of
Barnhill on the
A534.

Cheshire's Maiden Castle is perhaps not as well known nationally as the one in Dorset, but it is fairly impressive all the same. It is the best preserved of a series of seven such earthworks that run along the line of the Sandstone Trail down the middle of the county, the more notable others being Kellsborrow Castle at Kelsall and Eddisbury Castle near Delamere.

There are two semi-circular earthen ramparts that are very visible. Originally, they would have had a height of about 10ft each and a width of about 20ft. Their design was semi-circular along the eastern flank of the hill. On the western side, no defensive works were needed due to the steepness of the ridge sides. At the entrance, the walls curve inwards to provide additional protection at the fort's weakest point.

The fort was probably started in the first century BC, although the outer rampart seems to have been further fortified between AD 50 and AD 75, possibly as a means of resisting the advances of the Romans through Britain at this time. A small settlement was established below the fort, but all had been abandoned by the end of the first century AD.

Excavations carried out in the early 1930s discovered a small piece of iron, helping to date the fort and confirm that the locals had knowledge of iron before the Romans arrived.

In his monumental history of the county, compiled in 1816-19, George Ormerod, the Cheshire historian and antiquary, described the castle as 'one of the most perfect specimens of British castramentation in Cheshire'.

AN ELEGANT AND HISTORIC BRIDGE LINKING TWO COUNTRIES

FARNDON OR HOLT BRIDGE, FARNDON

The twin villages of Farndon (in England) and Holt (in Wales) enjoy a friendly rivalry. They are linked by this elegant and historic bridge. Unfortunately, a single name for it cannot be agreed!

The bridge was built in 1338 by John, Earl of Warenne, and contained a fortified gateway. In 1627 it was described as having ten arches, with a tower gatehouse on the fifth arch from the Welsh side, which contained a Lady Chapel. This arch, actually the third from the Holt side, is known as the 'Lady's Arch', and has additional strengthening above the main arch.

In 1643, the bridge was the site of a minor battle in the Civil War. The Parliamentarians, under Sir William Brereton, were trying to cross the bridge in a bid to encircle the Royalist-held Chester, but it was defended by Welsh loyal to the King. However, on 7 December, Brereton undertook a decoy operation a mile downstream, which drew some of the Royalist defenders away from the bridge. A direct attack on the uplifted drawbridge with ladders led to its ropes being cut and the bridge lowered. The remaining Welshmen were scattered after some grenades were thrown, thus enabling the Parliamentary forces to gain access to North Wales.

Access

From the centre of Farndon via the High Street.

ONE OF THE OLDEST CHURCHES IN CHESHIRE

ST EDITH'S CHURCH, SHOCKLACH

Access

At the end of Church Lane, which leads off the unclassified road westwards about 1.5 miles north of the village.

This small Norman church, located at the end of a quiet lane, is one of the oldest ecclesiastical buildings in Cheshire. It is constructed in delightful red sandstone and dates from about 1150. Originally, the village it served would have been in the immediate locality, but it is likely to have been moved around the time of the Black Death.

The nave is dedicated to St Edith, who is presumed to have been a daughter of the tenth-century Saxon king, Edward the Elder.

The church contains a hatchment or 'mourning board' (another is located at Burton church on the Wirral). This one commemorates the Pulestone family, who were patrons of the parish in its early days.

A CHURCH WITH A PULPIT SUPPORTED BY A TREE STUMP

ST CHAD'S CHURCH, TUSHINGHAM

This brick and slate church is another located in the midst of green fields, and bears an air of dignified simplicity. It was built in 1689-91 and probably replaced an earlier wooden structure that is believed to have stood on the site for over 300 years.

Originally, the church would have been next to the main Whitchurch to Chester road, but the road was diverted when improvements to the highway were carried out. The old line of the road is no longer evident.

Inside there is a panelled pulpit, supported on one side by a tree stump, which also acts as a seat for the reader of the lessons. There is also a movable oak font and a gallery and staircase provided in 1827 by the Vaudrey family.

In the corner of the graveyard stands a small brick building, built in 1822 for use as a meeting room. However, its main use, particularly in the later nineteenth century, would have been as a hearse house, when the local 'Black Maria' would have been kept by the parish to bring the dead to church. The actual horse-drawn hearse, built in 1880, is still kept in the building, and would have been used here up to about 1920, when firms of undertakers became more commonplace.

The church was replaced in 1863 when a 'new' church was built next to the current main road.

Like Forest Chapel near Macclesfield, this church is the site of an annual Rushbearing service.

Access

Via a field footpath which leads off Old Chad's Lane, itself off the eastern side of the A49 about 3 miles north of Whitchurch.

THE CENTRE OF AUDLEM'S PAST ACTIVITIES

BUTTERMARKET, AUDLEM

Access

In the main square, fronting St James's Church.

Sometimes called the Market Hall or the Shambles, this simple structure, adorned by eight Tuscan pillars, and with a floor of crazy paving, was built (or reconstructed) in 1733.

As a market place, it was never very successful, although an attempt was made to revive it in 1817. In 1906, it was being used for auctions. At a later date, the last attempt at revival took the form of two individuals, a man and a woman, who for many years would meet here once a week at 3 p.m. He would bring a wicker basket of food and she would be waiting for his produce. After about five minutes of 'trading', the 'market' would be over! The market rights were finally acquired by the local parish council in 1939 for the sum of £5. Now containing seating benches, it was restored in 1992.

Nearby, is a large granite block, to which was formerly attached an iron ring. This is called the Bear Stone and is probably a glacial 'erratic' or boulder carried a long distance by glaciers, in this case from Cumbria or the Mourne Mountains in Northern Ireland.

Bears would have been tethered to it in the days when bear baiting was allowed. Prizes would be awarded to the best dogs who could pin the bear by its nose. Unlike in cockfighting, the bear was never killed. The last 'bearward', the man responsible for the bear, was called Billy Borf.

The stone originally occupied the centre of the Square, but it was displaced when the lamp standard and monument to Richard Baker Bellyse, a doctor who served Audlem for forty years in the Victorian era, was erected in 1879.

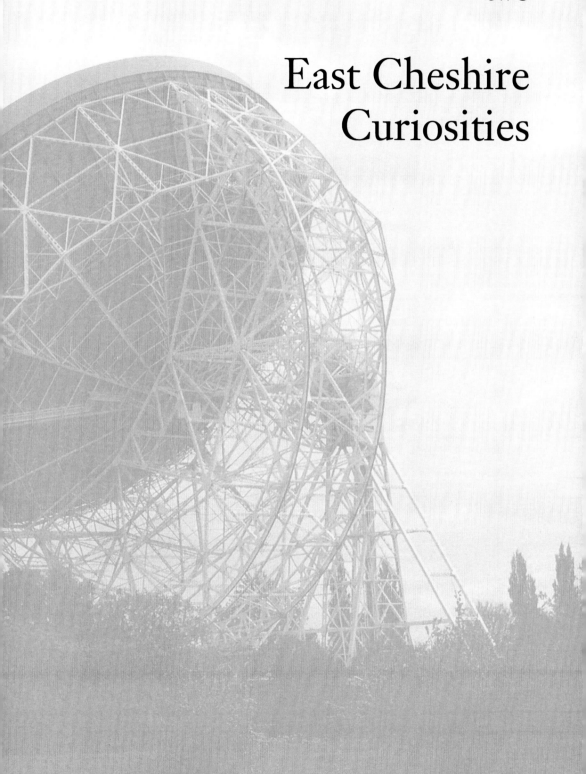

two

East Cheshire Curiosities

JUST WHAT WAS THE PURPOSE OF THESE STONES?

THE BOWSTONES, DISLEY

Access

At Bowstone-gate Farm, which is at the end of a minor road leading off the road leading from Disley to Kettleshulme (Mudhurst Lane).

These two upright stones are said to be of late Saxon origin. For a long time, it was thought that they were long-standing boundary markers or landmarks, but more recent research has contended that they were originally part of the Saxon crosses that were located in Disley up to the time of the Reformation.

Two stone cross heads were found during ploughing in a field near Disley church in about 1845, and a twin-socketed stone base was found close to the church in 1956. The cross heads are now kept at Lyme Hall. The Bowstones are identical in style, measurements and embellishments to both the cross heads and the base.

It appears that the two crosses in Disley churchyard were dismantled about 1548 following the Reformation, and that the shafts were set up at their present

location some time before 1590, possibly by Sir Piers Legh of Lyme, who died that year. Whether they were meant to be guide posts, boundary stones or wayside shrines, or all of these, is not known.

Another theory is that the shafts themselves were placed in their present position on Park Moor in the seventeenth or eighteenth centuries.

WHERE POACHERS USED TO BE 'CAGED'

LYME CAGE, LYME PARK

Set prominently on a ridge, Lyme Cage is said to have its origins from around 1524. One theory holds that it was built even earlier, during the Wars of the Roses, as a watch tower. One of its early uses was to apprehend poachers before being taken for trial, which is probably why it has acquired its name.

In 1733-7, it was reconstructed to a design by the Italian architect, Giacomo Leoni, who was engaged in reconstruction work on Lyme Hall at the time. At around 848ft above sea level, it is said that Lyme Cage was also used as a vantage point for hunting or military purposes (the Home Guard used it during the Second World War).

It was latterly occupied by estate keepers (who lived in the upper floors) until about 1920 and it was bricked up in around 1947, when the park was taken over by the National Trust and Stockport Corporation.

Three of the elevations contain sundials (giving the time by Greenwich Mean Time) with inscriptions in Latin or English. It is rumoured that an underground passage links the Cage with the Hall, but there appears to be no evidence in support of this.

Some restoration work was carried out in the late 1980s, followed by a more complete scheme ten years later. The interior is now open on alternate Sunday afternoons.

Access

Easily visible to the left of the main entrance driveway to the Hall.

THIS BUILDING USED TO STAND ON TOP OF LYME HALL

THE LANTERN, LYME PARK

Access

Some way
from the main
features of
Lyme Park,
in the centre
of Lantern
Wood, which
is located on
rising land to
the eastern
edges of the
park.

Located on rising ground towards the eastern edges of the park is this curious structure known as the Lantern.

Sometimes called the Lanthorn Tower, this structure is less well known than Lyme Cage. Its name derives from its shape: three storeys in height with a triangular roof, with an archway on the lowest floor.

It was originally located on the roof of the Elizabethan Lyme Hall, but was taken down and re-erected here, as a focal point, when Giacomo Leoni was undertaking his alterations to the Hall in the eighteenth century.

In recent years, some restoration of the stonework has taken place and visitors can now access the interior.

REMAINS OF POYNTON'S INDUSTRIAL PAST

RAILWAY INCLINES, POYNTON

The commuter area of Poynton is not recognised by many today as being an industrial area, but it was the centre of a coal mining district until 1935. Several deep-level mines operated to the east of the village.

A system of colliery railways linked the mines to the main Stockport to Macclesfield railway line. Today, overgrown colliery spoil heaps remain at the eastern side of the village, some old mine buildings at the former Anson Pit, and a few other reminders.

A significant feature was the two lengthy cable worked inclines, the Princes and the Lady's Inclines, both of which ran from Tower Road towards London Road. These can both be walked today and are pleasantly tree-lined. They dated from the 1840s and replaced an earlier system of narrow gauge colliery tramways.

Those wishing to explore more of Poynton's industrial past are advised to visit the Anson Engine Museum, located in some of the buildings of Poynton's last coal mine, Anson Pit, on Anson Road. It was set up some years ago by Geoff Challinor and Les Cawley, both enthusiasts of static industrial engines.

Access

Via Woodside, on the eastern side of London Road (A523), a few hundred yards north of the town centre.

A VERY EFFICIENT AND ECONOMICAL DRINKING FOUNTAIN

ORNAMENTAL LAMP POST AND FOUNTAIN, POYNTON

Access

On the traffic island opposite Poynton church, at the junction of London Road (A523) and Chester Road (A5143).

This ornate cast-iron lamp post and drinking fountain was erected by the people of Poynton in commemoration of Queen Victoria's Diamond Jubilee in 1897.

Provided by Wilson & Co. of Manchester at a cost of £212, it combines the functions of lamp post, direction sign and drinking fountain. The lamps are still operational, though no longer lit by gas, but he fountain no longer functions, its features now being filled with carefully tended floral displays.

On three sides of the central plinth are lion masks. These would have produced, when operational, a jet of water that fed, respectively, a square basin for human use, a semi-circular basin for use by horses, and finally a bowl for dogs.

Another ornamental fountain, this time a stone one, can be found in the centre of the nearby village of Disley, in Fountain Square.

To the north of Poynton, on the eastern side of London Road North (A523), about half a mile north of the town centre, is Poynton Lake. This lake, often unseen by motorists speeding along the main road here, is not a natural lake, but was dug as part of Poynton Park by Sir George Warren in the late eighteenth century, and is in effect a reservoir. The road itself is situated on the dam wall.

The park was acquired by the local authority in the 1930s. Within the park are two lime trees, each well over 300 years old, which mark the position of the old entrance driveway to the former Poynton Hall.

WHERE HANDEL PLAYED THE ORGAN

'FATHER SMITH' ORGAN, ADLINGTON HALL

Adlington Hall, an attractive manor house in brick and black-and-white timbering, has been home to the Legh family since 1315. The timber parts of the building date mainly from the sixteenth century, including the Great Hall, completed in 1605.

The most striking features of the Great Hall are the twin oak trees supporting the east end, each carved into an octagonal shape, which are said to have been the two original oak trees around which the first building, a hunting lodge, was built. They are said to have been left in situ in the spot where they grew.

Between them is one of the finest seventeenth-century organs in the country, reputedly built by 'Father' Bernard Smith around 1690, and thought to have been played by George Frederick Handel when he visited his friends, the Leghs, in 1741-42, and possibly again in 1748. The instrument terminates in a splendid flourish with the family coat of arms, surmounted by their white unicorn crest, set between trumpeting angels, celebrating the marriage of John Legh (1668-1739) to Isabella Robartes in 1693.

The organ possesses two manuals (keyboards), but no pedal board. It became unplayable in about 1805, but was restored by Noel Mander in 1958-9 and can today be heard on special occasions. No other organs in the UK from this era survive in their original condition and location. It has been described as 'a breathtaking example of the organmaker's art, unlike anything else in England'.

Access

Via Mill Lane, which is to the west of the Stockport to Macclesfield road (A523) at the Legh Arms crossroads. Adlington Hall is open on Sunday and Wednesday afternoons in July and August.

AN ARISTOCRATIC FOLLY

SHELL COTTAGE, ADLINGTON HALL

Access

As previously.

The grounds and gardens of Adlington Hall, said to have been laid out by the Legh family in the mid-eighteenth century in the style of 'Capability' Brown, are graced with a number of architectural features at focal points.

This Shell Cottage, built in the mid-eighteenth century (though the shells on the interior were not added until about a hundred years later) is the only example of such a feature near the Greater Manchester conurbation, although they are commonly found at other locations in the UK. Access to the interior is not now possible, but a good view can be had by looking through the windows.

Adjoining the formal gardens to the east is the 'Wilderness' where can be found a Classical rotunda-like 'Temple to Diana', complete with painted ceiling, a 'Rat House', and a ruined Hermitage.

A LITTLE PIECE OF BROADCASTING HISTORY

ROMANY'S CARAVAN, WILMSLOW

This old gypsy caravan, or 'vardo', represents a piece of broadcasting history. It formerly belonged to the Revd George Bramwell Evens, who, from 1932 until his death at the age of 59 in November 1943, featured as 'Romany' in what was one of the most popular BBC radio programmes of the time, *Children's Hour.*

Descended from gypsy stock himself, Evens was an experienced public speaker, and the often unscripted programmes and excellent sound effects convinced many listeners that the programmes were actually broadcast out on the open road. He had bought the vardo in 1921 from the gypsy fair at Brough and it had been on many trips around Yorkshire, Cumberland and Westmorland.

Before he went into broadcasting, Evens had been writing nature articles for local newspapers in Yorkshire. This encouraged a friend in 1931 to arrange an audition for him for the programme *Children's Hour*. On his retirement from the Methodist Church in September 1939, he came to live in Wilmslow to be near the BBC's Manchester studios.

The caravan was given to the local authority by his widow after his death. The current garden was laid out in 1950 with the memorial stone being unveiled by his former colleagues, Muriel Levy and Doris Gamball (who had played the parts of young girls in the programmes). Close by is the small grave of his beloved dog, Raq, who died in 1947. The garden was given an overhaul in 1992.

The caravan is open for public viewing on the second Saturday of each month between May and September.

Access

Off South Drive, behind Hoopers department store and opposite Wilmslow Library.

A REMARKABLE ESTATE VILLAGE

STYAL VILLAGE, QUARRY BANK MILL AND STYAL CROSS

Access

Car parking is located either to the south of Altrincham Road, which leads westwards off the B5166, or in the main car park off Quarry Bank Road.

Quarry Bank Mill, established by Samuel Greg in 1784, and its adjacent estate village have long been popular destinations, especially since the opening of the mill to the public in the late 1970s.

Greg established his mill at Styal to take advantage of available water power from the River Bollin. Building the mill in what then would have been a relatively isolated area would have been impossible without the willingness of the Gregs to provide housing for the workforce. The village of Styal, now the responsibility of the National Trust, remains the perfect example of the self-contained industrial community, with its Co-operative shop, Apprentice House, schools and chapels.

The remains of Styal Cross (pictured), have been on this site within the village since July 1981. It was originally located on Styal Green and for many years stood at the junction of Altrincham Road and Holly Lane, until it was demolished by a rather careless motorist some thirty years ago.

Nearby, a 'fake' stone circle stands to the east of the entrance driveway to Norcliffe Hall, which was built by Robert Hyde Greg, the son of Samuel Greg, in 1831, with further additions in 1870. (Access is not possible as Norcliffe Hall is private, but a rather distant view may be obtained from the Altrincham Road entrance.)

Robert Hyde Greg had developed an interest in antiquities through accompanying his father on business trips to Europe and the Middle East, and this stone circle was placed in the grounds by him.

JUST WHAT IS MEANT BY THIS INSCRIPTION?

WIZARD WELL, ALDERLEY EDGE

Carved into the rock face beside the footpath is the bearded face of a wizard, below which are the following words:

DRINK OF THIS
AND TAKE THY FILL
FOR THE WATER FALLS
BY THE WIZHARD'S WILL

The origin of this feature is obscure, but it is clearly related to the often told tale of a local farmer, led by the wizard through a set of iron gates into the hillside, where he was obliged to sell his horse to one of a group of sleeping knights, who were waiting to be summoned to save their country in a time of great trouble.

The story is believed to have originated in the middle of the seventeenth century, although it did not appear in print until 1805. With the development of Alderley Edge as a commuter town for the rapidly growing Manchester in the mid-nineteenth century, the myths and legends associated with the Edge began to have a wider audience.

Alderley Edge novelist, Alan Garner (author of the best-selling *The Weirdstone of Brisingamen*), claims that the feature was carved by his great-great-grandfather, Robert Garner, in the nineteenth century as an embellishment to the many myths and legends associated with the Edge.

Elsewhere on the Edge are other wells, of some antiquity, called respectively the Holy Well, Mermaid's Pool and Wishing Well.

Nearby, located just off the path leading from Beacon Hill to the Holy Well and Stormy Point, are the Druid Stones. This stone circle was for many years thought to have been a Druidical cromlech of considerable age.

It is now believed to have been built as a small folly, possibly during the nineteenth century. It is another feature that Alan Garner says originated with his forebear Robert Garner, who simply wanted to find a use for some old stones!

Access

Park in the lay-by on Macclesfield Road (B5087) and walk down the path to the Edge. Take the footpath that leads down to the left. After a minute's walk, the well can be seen on the left.

A UNIQUE GALLERY PEW

NETHER ALDERLEY CHURCH

Access

Just off the
Congleton
Road (A34)
opposite
Nether
Alderley Mill.

Inside this attractive church is a unique Jacobean gallery box pew provided for the exclusive use of the local lords of the manor, the Stanley family. Access to this is via an outside staircase. The panelling contains the family's coat-of-arms, and the pew, looking a bit like a theatre 'box', has an ornately decorated plaster ceiling.

The church has arrow grooves in the stonework of its south porch. The churchyard is circular in shape, indicating its origin for defensive purposes in Saxon times. In the churchyard is the imposing Stanley Mausoleum, built in 1909,

and the former schoolroom. The latter was erected by the Revd Hugo Shaw in 1628, with teaching space on the ground floor, and an upper floor for the schoolmaster's use. It was described in 1700 by Francis Gastrey, then Bishop of Chester, in his 'Notitia Cestriensis'. It was restored in 1909 by the Rt Hon. E.C. Stanley, the fourth Baron Stanley of Alderley, for the parish council to use as a parish hall, in which use it remains today.

A CHAPEL WITH TWO PUBLIC FACES

BAPTIST CHAPEL, GREAT WARFORD

This chapel shows two contrasting faces, with a 'public face' to the road, but an untouched rear showing what is clearly the timber construction of an early Tudor barn, with its wattle and daub replaced by brick infilling.

Following the Toleration Act, Dissenting Chapels could be licensed, and in 1712 a cottage and adjoining barn were acquired and converted into the building seen today. This was to serve a local congregation, formed from local Puritans, who had been meeting in secret since 1668, latterly in Pownall Brow Farm, about a mile to the north.

At a later date, the building was divided and the western half became a house. The furniture in the remaining half is all original, apart from the electronic organ!

Access

On the northern side of Merryman's Lane, about half a mile to the west of Chelford Road (A535).

INFLUENCES OF ITALY AND ISLAM IN KNUTSFORD

WATT'S MINARET, KNUTSFORD

Access

Located on the south side of Drury Lane, close to the town centre.

This so-called Minaret was originally a water tower to a steam laundry complex. Built in 1899 for the Knutsford Steam Laundry, the Minaret is one example of the influence on Knutsford of the wealthy and eccentric Manchester glove manufacturer, Richard Harding Watt.

Watt had travelled extensively, and was strongly influenced by Islamic and Italian buildings, as well as by the work of William Morris and others in the Arts and Crafts Movement.

The laundry complex was designed for Watt by the Manchester architect, Henry Fairhurst, but Watt's influence on the style is clear. The Minaret originally had a roof structure with a small spire, and is said to have been influenced by a tower in Damascus that he had seen.

The name 'Minaret' is a bit of a misnomer as it is square in appearance. The laundry complex originally possessed a tower, now demolished, which was shaped like a true Islamic minaret.

Today, the laundry complex has been converted into attractive if unusual residences, the Minaret being called the 'Tower House'.

On the corner of Drury Lane and Ruskin Court are the Ruskin Rooms, built by Watt in 1902 as a leisure and educational facility for the townspeople of Knutsford. Designed by Walter Aston in a mixture of Mediterranean, Islamic and Art Nouveaux styles, it has had a variety of uses over the years, including fire station and British Legion headquarters. During 1944-45, it served as a 'Welcome Club' for US forces stationed in the area. Following restoration in 1977, it has been used as offices.

BUILT TO COMMEMORATE THE AUTHOR OF *CRANFORD*

GASKELL MEMORIAL TOWER, KNUTSFORD

Along with the Minaret (see previous), there are other Richard Harding Watt-influenced buildings in the town of Knutsford. A group of houses on Legh Road have a very distinctive style. Some years ago they featured in a television drama series as colonial houses in inter-war Shanghai.

However, the best known example of Watt's architecture, and the focal point of the town's main street, is the Gaskell Memorial Tower and the adjacent Bell Epoque Restaurant. Both were built by Watt in 1907/8, in memory of Mrs Elizabeth Gaskell, the novelist who lived for many years in the town, and who immortalised it in her novel *Cranford*.

The Tower contains three copper bells, each bearing an inscription. A bas-relief and a bust of the authoress also feature, together with a carved list of her main works and quotations from Milton, Cromwell, Gladstone and others.

The adjoining restaurant was originally the King's Coffee House, provided to serve non-alcoholic drinks to the local townspeople. For a time it was used by Knutsford Urban District Council.

The adjacent side courtyard is worth a look, featuring as it does two impressive white pillars which were rescued by Watt when Manchester's St Peter's Church, formerly in St Peter's Square, was demolished in 1907.

Access

On the western side of King Street, in the town centre.

ONCE THE HOME OF A NOTORIOUS HIGHWAYMAN AND BURGLAR

HEATH HOUSE, KNUTSFORD

Access

Close to the junction of Ladies Mile and Tabley Road, to the north west of the town centre.

This house, now divided into several dwellings, has had a distinguished history. It is now known as 'Heath House', but has been known as 'Heathfield', and prior to that 'Cann Office House', the latter being the name for a location where weights and measures were officially verified, quite a problem in times past.

However, this house's most memorable period is the decade in the mid-eighteenth century when it was home to Edward Higgins, a noted housebreaker and highwayman.

Higgins early criminal career saw him accused of sheep stealing. A later housebreaking sentence saw him transported to America for seven years, but he returned to England with funds raised after breaking into a house in Boston. By 1757 he was living in Knutsford.

In the following years, Higgins endeared himself to the local well-to-do inhabitants, hunting 'with them during the morning, dined with them in the afternoon, and made himself familiar with their plate chests by night' according to Henry Green, a nineteenth-century Knutsford historian. Every year, Higgins would leave the town for a month or two, to collect the 'rents' from his country estates. In reality, he was commiting crimes in far-off counties. It was on one of these trips, at Carmarthen in 1767, that he was finally caught.

He was convicted and hanged on 7 November, though true to his form, he attempted to escape his punishment by having a friend deliver a forged pardon. His wife and children were unaware of his 'other life' but he did leave behind a confession for all his crimes, including murder.

A MYTHOLOGICAL CONNECTION TO ROSTHERNE MERE

MERMAID'S HEAD, ROSTHERNE CHURCHYARD

This small carved head is possibly up to 2,000 years old, and is thought to be the ancient god Cernunnos, who inhabited lakes and springs, and who had a fish-like tail, mermaid style.

Local mythology has a mermaid inhabiting Rostherne Mere, the deepest lake in Cheshire, at over 100ft deep in places. The Mere is also rumoured to be linked to the sea in some way, a legend supported by the fact that until the early 1920s, the Mere was home to Smelt, a type of fish usually only found in salt water.

The Mere is a local nature reserve, noted for its visiting birds. Public access is extremely limited.

While in the area, have a look at Rostherne village, a picturesque 'estate village', part of the Tatton Estate.

Access

The church is on the northern side of the village. It is set at the corner of the retaining walls on the side of the church nearest the Mere.

A LOCK-UP FOR SHEEP THIEVES OR A SHEEPWATCHER'S TOWER?

SHEEP STEALERS TOWER, TATTON PARK

Access

Main access
is via the
A5034 and
Ashley Road.
Admission
charge
payable.

Tatton Park is one of the National Trust's most visited properties. The extensive gardens are the location of several follies erected by the Egerton family, who owned the park until 1957.

This tower, found in a small garden called the Tower Garden, was built before 1750. It is two storeys high, and contains a fireplace and water supply, indicating its possible use as a residence at some time. In days gone by, it was not unknown for the aristocracy to allow hermits to live on their estates and this tower could have been used for such a purpose. Sometimes, the general idea was to give the host's visitors a bit of a fright!

Its name is said to derive from stories of sheep thieves being locked up in it, but other claims suggest that it is similar to the sheepwatchers' towers formerly found in Cumbria and Yorkshire.

Nearby, on a small island in the Japanese Garden, is a wooden Shinto temple. Created in 1910 along with the rest of the Japanese Garden by Alan de Tatton, it was transported from Japan and erected by Japanese workmen brought in to landscape the garden.

AN EXAMPLE OF THE ARISTOCRACY'S LIKING FOR THE CLASSICAL

CHORAGIC MONUMENT TO LYSICRATES, TATTON PARK

Access

As previously.

This rotunda-like monument is located at the end of the Broad Walk in the gardens. It was commissioned by Wilbraham Egerton in 1820, and built by William Cole III, a pupil of the Chester architect, Thomas Harrison.

Originally, the monument was surrounded by a balustrade and steps, as if on a platform. These were removed in 1965 after damage was caused by subsidence from brine extraction activities in the Cheshire saltfield.

The monument is one of many British copies of the monument to the famous chorus (i.e. Storyteller) Lysicrates in Ancient Greece. It stands overlooking Melchett Mere, a body of water formed through subsidence caused by brine extraction. The Mere is still increasing in size as a result of this process. It was named after one of the former luminaries of the county's salt extraction business.

The last Lord Egerton, Maurice, used the monument to warn walkers coming onto the estate from Knutsford that they should not cross an imaginary line that led from it to a flagpole at one end of Melchett Mere.

Located nearby, between Melchett Mere and the Choragic Monument, is an ice house. Used in pre-refrigeration days, ice houses were often to be found on the estates of the wealthy and were used to store the ice collected in the winter from the estates' lakes. The ice could be kept for up to two years if properly treated and sealed with straw.

In around 1880, the ice house was replaced by another closer to Tatton Hall, and it was used to store silage instead.

REMINDERS OF THE 'RHYMING SQUIRE'

ROWLAND EGERTON-WARBURTON'S SIGNS, ARLEY ESTATE

Access

This particular sign is located at the junction of Sack Lane and Carr Lane, about a mile from the Arley Hall, but more may be found around the estate.

Rowland Eyles Egerton-Warburton (1804-1891) was known as the 'Rhyming Squire' of Arley after the many amusing poems and songs that he wrote, some of which were used on signboards on the Arley Estate. Sometimes, these amusing ditties have a serious intent, for example to deter trespassers.

Educated at Eton and Oxford, he settled on his estate after undertaking the customary Grand Tour of Europe, and set out developing his holdings, including rebuilding Arley Hall with the house that stands today.

His talents for songs and poetry really got going in 1846, when a collection of his works, written for the Tarporley Hunt Club, of which he was a keen member, was published as *Hunting Songs*. This was republished eight times before his death, and occasionally in subsequent years.

The present-day signposts are copies of the original versions.

A COLLECTION OF PRESTBURY'S CURIOSITIES

NORMAN CHAPEL AND FORMER PARSONAGE, PRESTBURY

The name Prestbury is understood to be Saxon for 'Priest's Town'. In the churchyard of Prestbury church is this Norman chapel, the predecessor of the current parish church. The chapel dates from the end of the twelfth century, being no doubt built on the site of an earlier Saxon church. The western elevation is the most interesting, with a row of carved figures above the doorway. Above this is a Latin inscription stating that the chapel was restored in 1747 by Sir William Meredith of Macclesfield. The present glass in the windows was only installed, however, in 1977.

On the main church building's south porch, itself dating from 1220, can be seen grooves caused when arrows were being sharpened in medieval times. The arrows were made from the yew trees grown in the churchyard. In the churchyard are parts of an ancient cross believed to date from AD 670, that were discovered embedded in the chancel wall on 1841. A large part of the head is missing. It is thought the cross commemorates the arrival of Christianity in the area.

Across the road from the church is the black-and-white building that is now the National Westminster Bank. This building, dating from the sixteenth century, was previously the local parsonage. Local tradition maintains that the balcony over the doorway was used by the priest during the period of the Commonwealth, when he would have been barred from preaching in the church.

When a new parsonage was built in 1708, the building was divided into cottages. Shortly before the First World War, the building was declared unfit for housing use and it later became an antique shop. It was completely restored between 1968 and 1970, when it became a bank.

Access

On the main road in the centre of the village.

HOW DID THIS FOLLY GET ITS NAME?

WHITE NANCY, BOLLINGTON

Access

Located on
Redway, one
of the roads
between
Bollington and
Kerridge.

This white-painted structure is in the shape of a sugar loaf with a white ball finial on its top. It is some 920ft above sea level and is visible from miles around, sometimes being said to be used by pilots approaching Manchester Airport.

It was originally a folly or summerhouse, and contained a circular stone table and stone benches around the perimeter. Other theories are that it was a lovers' meeting place or a place for quiet meditation.

How the structure originated and how it gained it name has been the subject of much speculation. The favourite story is that it was constructed in 1817 by the Gaskell family of the nearby North End Farm and Ingersley Hall to commemorate the victory at Waterloo, and was named after one of the ladies of the family. An alternative is that it was named after the horse leading the team of eight that pulled the large stone up the hill to form the central table. Yet another story is that the name is a play on the word 'ordnance', as in Ordnance Survey (there is an OS triangulation column at the southern end of Kerridge Hill). However, this theory is considered rather less likely as the Ordnance Survey did not begin to survey the area until the 1840s, and the structure had been referred to as 'Northern Nancy' in 1825.

Bonfires were lit here to celebrate Queen Victoria's Golden Jubilee, and the Coronations of Edward VIII and George V in 1902 and 1911. Its entrance was sealed in the 1930s.

THE SECOND HIGHEST PUBLIC HOUSE IN ENGLAND

CAT & FIDDLE INN

This public house was built by Macclesfield banker, John Ryle, in 1830, a few years after the new road between Macclesfield and Buxton was constructed, and became a frequent stopping place for tourist wagonettes taking the route.

At 1,690ft above sea level, it is said to be the second highest public house in England – the Tan Hill Inn in Yorkshire's Swaledale being the highest, although counter claims are made from time to time.

How exactly the pub got its name is not known. It might be simply taken from the nursery rhyme of the same name. Other suggestions are it came from Catherine Fidelis (after Catherine of Aragon, Henry VIII's first wife), 'Caton le Fidele' (a governor of Calais), a derivation of 'le chat fidele' ('the faithful cat'), or after the old game of 'trap ball', where a tapered stick called a 'cat' was used, and which could have been accompanied by playing fiddlers. An 1886 guide states that it was one of the favourite rides of the Duke of Devonshire, the owner of Chatsworth. He used to bring with him his favourite Angora cat whom he once seated by a fiddle for the purposes of a photograph, which he then presented to the landlord.

The pub is a popular place at weekends for the biking community, who are attracted by the challenges of the winding road up from Macclesfield, often referred to as the 'Cat & Fiddle Road'. The road, not surprisingly, is also a great favourite with the local traffic police!

Access

On the A537 between Macclesfield and Buxton.

WHY HAS THIS CHAPEL RECEIVED ITS NAME?

JENKIN CHAPEL, SALTERSFORD

Access

At the junction of Bank Lane and Hooleyhey Lane on the unclassified road linking Rainow and the Errwood Reservoirs.

This Church of England chapel is built in a very isolated and exposed location. It was dedicated in June 1733 to St John the Baptist, and remains almost in its original state, untouched by Victorian 'restorations'. It was partly financed by John Slack of nearby Salterford Hall.

In the early eighteenth century this location was a stopping point on the old salt route from North Wales to Derbyshire, also used by cattle drovers and sheep stealers. An ancient track marking stone became known as Jenkin's Cross, possibly named after a man named Jenkin from Ruthin who regularly carried out business here, or from a fiery preacher who preached at the horse fair which took place at this spot. Other theories are that Jenkin was the name of a local farming family, or that because a large proportion of the money to build the church was raised through voluntary contributions, the name arose from 'jinking', the sound made by charity collectors to this day when they shake their collecting tins!

The building today appears crude, and is very like a farmhouse, being provided with two rows of Georgian cottage windows and a chimney stack. A small tower was added in 1754-5, which, when completed, was celebrated with a 'roaring feast', with ale provided to the value of *2s 6d*. The church was not officially consecrated until 1894, when it was re-dedicated to St John the Evangelist.

Access to the bell chamber and gallery is reached by a set of outside stone steps. Inside, the chapel still contains its original box pews, a high octagonal pulpit and a carved reading desk. The chancel is very small and was possibly added later.

One tombstone in the churchyard contains only the single word 'here', presumably because the family could not afford to have a full inscription carved.

A CURIOUS ALLEGORICAL GARDEN BASED ON *THE PILGRIM'S PROGRESS*

MELLOR'S GARDEN, RAINOW

James Mellor was just one year old in 1797 when he came to live at Hough Hole House. His father had built the local Methodist chapel in Rainow, and the young James quickly became involved in its Sunday school. He initially worked in his father's mill in the locality.

From the 1830s, James began to be influenced by the religious writings of Emanuel Swedenborg, although it is not known if he ever formally adopted the religion. The basis of Swedenborg's teaching is the 'Science of Correspondences' in which everything in the natural world has a counterpart in the spiritual world. The allegorical possibilities that garden design threw up became an important element of the religion.

Mellor started to develop his garden in the 1840s, and continued until his death in 1891, aged 95. The garden follows the theme of Bunyan's *The Pilgrims Progress*, and the names of the features, sometimes just a flight of steep steps (the 'Hill Difficulty'), or else a little building (the 'Celestial City'), follow those in the book, plus a few others, for example 'Uncle Tom's Cabin'.

Access

Off the Macclesfield–Whaley Bridge road (B5470). From the centre of the village, go eastwards via Round Mow and Sugar Lane and Hough Hole House is on the right after about half a mile.

The garden is testimony to Mellor's energy, inventiveness and practical skills, and was all his own work. Among the interesting features are many stone slabs bearing Biblical inscriptions and the unusual 'Howling House', which, when the door was open and the wind in the right direction, produced a strange eerie howling noise as the wind hit the strings of an Aeolian harp placed over a hole in the back wall (alas this feature does not now work).

The public were invited to visit the garden during Mellor's life, but after 1891, it was gradually forgotten. Restoration took place from 1978 to 1993, and today the gardens are opened on the late May and August Bank Holiday Mondays, from 2-5 p.m.

A MEMORIAL TO A MYSTERIOUS DEATH

JOHN TURNER MEMORIAL, RAINOW

This memorial stone, set in the road embankment, commemorates the mysterious death of John Turner, the 29-year-old son of Richard Turner of Saltersford Hall. John ran teams of mules and packhorses between Chester and Derby.

Christmas Eve 1735 saw John returning to be with his family for Christmas. By the time he had reached Bollington, the area had been gripped with a snowstorm and he was advised to go no further. But nevertheless he continued, with the result that he was frozen to death.

When a search party found him, the team of mules was found to be safe.

The stone, a second replacement for the original, which had been erected by James Mellor of Hough Hole House, tells the story on both sides:

Access

On the eastern side of Ewrin Lane, just below Buxter Stoops Farm.

Here John Turner was cast away in a heavy snowstorm in the night in or about the year 1755*

The print of a woman's shoe was found by his side in the snow where he lay dead. H

(* thought to be a mistake)

AN ISOLATED CHURCH NOTED FOR ITS RUSHBEARING CEREMONIES

FOREST CHAPEL, MACCLESFIELD FOREST

Access

Macclesfield Forest is a small hamlet reached by unclassified roads south of the A537, several miles east of Macclesfield.

This chapel was first built in 1673, and is believed to be dedicated to St Stephen, though this is not confirmed. It is constructed of sandstone and has a roof made from stone slates from the nearby Kerridge quarries. In about 1720, the Bishop of Chester remarked that the building had never been formally consecrated. The location of the chapel is very attractive.

Above the entrance are two carved stones, one with 'SS 1673' commemorating the building of the chapel, whilst the other marks the substantial re-building that took place in 1834.

The chapel's interior is very simple, but this is changed completely on the first Sunday after 12 August every year, when the building sees its annual rush bearing ceremony. This dates back to the days when churches had earthen floors and the dead were often buried within the church. At the ceremonies parishioners would bring sweet smelling rushes to strew within the church, to purify the air and help insulate the worshippers from the cold.

The service, which takes place at 3 p.m., attracts a congregation of over 600, with many hearing the service on a loudspeaker relay outside. Part way through the service, the priest and congregation go outside, where the sermon will be preached.

A similar service is held at St Chad's Church, Tushingham.

A MYSTERIOUS STONE CIRCLE IN A MAGNIFICENT SETTING

THE BULLSTONE, NEAR WINCLE

This ancient site, sometimes called the 'Bullstrang', comprises a headstone, approximately 4ft in height, set within a rough oval of cobbles about 8ft by 7ft. The oval is surrounded by a haphazard circle of slightly larger stones, about 20ft in diameter. Originally discovered by a Dr Sainter in 1878, the circle was believed to have an 'entrance' on the southern side, with further lines of stones that make out two rough narrow triangles on either side of it. Today, the lines of these features are difficult to make out with much certainty. The headstone itself is monolith-like, with a bowl-shaped depression on its top most likely caused by weathering.

The origin of this set of stones continues to puzzle archeologists and it defies classification. Some have suggested it was a round barrow, on account of the fact that Dr Sainter found in it the burnt bones of a young child along with a flint knife, arrowhead and an urn (now located in Congleton Museum). Others have suggested that it was a kerb circle or cairn, or that there was a more ceremonial function for the site. Similarities have been drawn with Bronze Age sites in South West Scotland, particularly one at Glenquickan.

What is not disputed is that this unobtrusive and quite modest monument is located on a truly outstanding site, with spectacular views of the surrounding parts of the Peak District to the north, east and south, including the striking summit of Shutlingsloe.

Nearby, on the A54, close to the Fourways Motel, stands Cleulow Cross. This is a tapering pillar of Millstone Grit about 10ft high, which stands on the top of an artificial low wooden hill. It is set in a block of stone 4ft square and 2ft deep. The Cross is on private land and close access is not possible.

Access

Take the A54 in the direction of Buxton. Park near the junction of Withenshaw Lane and the unclassified road that leads north off the A54 near the Fourways Motel. Take the public footpath leading South East from the road junction. After crossing two field stiles, the main stone is visible on the horizon to the right. For a closer look, cross the third stile, leave the (ill-defined) path, and climb the hill by circling round its southern side. Avoid disturbing grazing livestock, and remember to respect that this is private property.

CHESHIRE'S MOST IMPRESSIVE NEOLITHIC MONUMENT

THE BRIDESTONES

Access

On the south side of the hill known as The Cloud, on Dial Lane. Park on the main road and walk down the access road to the quarry. The entrance to the Bridestones is on the left.

This is perhaps Cheshire's most impressive ancient monument, albeit literally on the border with Staffordshire. It lies some 820ft above sea level and is on the western crest of a pass running north-south at this location. Its views over the Cheshire plain are spectacular.

What is there today is a shadow of its former self. As late as 1760, it was described as being 110 metres long and 11 metres wide, containing three separate compartments, only one of which remains today. Originally, the cairn, dating from the Neolithic Stone Age, was surrounded by a circle of stones, of which only two survive. Unusually for such a structure in this locality, it has a paved crescent forecourt.

Why they are called the Bridestones is unclear. One myth is that a newly married couple was murdered at the site, and that the stones were their grave. Or was it a reference to Brigantia? The Old English word for birds was 'briddes', and the original shape of the monument might have suggested this.

In the later eighteenth and early nineteenth centuries, the monument was robbed of many of its stones for local buildings and the nearby turnpike road. The broken cross slab on the remaining chamber, originally 18ft long, was split by a picnicker's bonfire in 1843.

Manchester University excavated the site in 1936-37. It is currently in need of some care, attention and recognition.

A CHURCH WITH THREE DISTINCTIVE TYPES OF CONSTRUCTION

ALL SAINTS' CHURCH, SIDDINGTON

This church has a distinctive appearance. The west wall of the tower appears black-and-white timber framing, but is in fact just a pattern painted on the brickwork.

The nave appears to be plain brickwork, but in reality this brickwork covers timber framing. When the roof of the church was being renewed in 1815, the heavy Kerridge tiles used proved too be too heavy for the existing timber framing dating from the fourteenth and fifteenth centuries. The timber framing was therefore encased in brick, and can still be seen inside the church in places where the plasterwork has been removed to expose it. The chancel and south porch are genuine timber framing.

The church had a single bell installed in 1588, the year of the Spanish Armada, to warn of any impending invasion.

In the churchyard is a single yew tree, believed to be as old as the church itself. The yew trees were grown to provide timber for arrows. These trees could only be grown in churchyards, as their berries were poisonous to animals, who were not allowed in the churchyards.

On the last Saturday in July, the Redesmere Fête takes place in the nearby village hall. The fête begins when the Waterlily Queen is rowed across the nearby Redesmere in a swan-shaped boat for her coronation.

Access

Off the south side of Pexhill Road (B5392), just east of its junction with the A34.

THE RESTING PLACE OF 'LORD FLAME'

MAGGOTY JOHNSON'S GRAVE, GAWSWORTH

Access

At the junction of Maggoty Lane and Church Lane, about half a mile north of Gawsworth village.

These two stones mark the grave of Samuel Johnson, or 'Old Maggoty' as he was known by some; said to be the last professional jester in England.

Born in Cheshire in 1691, he spent his early career teaching dancing to the local gentry, but his natural gifts of poetry, wit, music and acting soon encouraged a move to London. In 1729, he took the part of 'Lord Flame' in his own play, called 'Hurlothrumbo, or the Supernatural', which was the talk of the year. Further works followed, but he was never to repeat this success.

By the early 1740s, he had returned to Cheshire, living in part of the New Hall at Gawsworth, at the invitation of the Earl of Harrington, to whom he had once been dancing-master. He referred to himself as Lord Flame, and his supporters would send their donations to New Hall, where they would be presented to Johnson once a year with the words, 'My Lord, I have brought you your rents.' In return, he would write out an official receipt. In the locality, his wit was popular with the local gentry, and it is from this era that his reputation as the last jester derives. However, by others he was called 'Old Maggoty', indicating a rather more decrepit and idiosyncratic individual.

In his later years, he loved to walk in this wood and stated his wish to be buried there, in unconsecrated ground. He died in 1773, and his gravestone (the left-hand stone) is carved with his own amusing epitaph. The other stone dates from 1851, when Lady Harrington, disapproving of Old Maggoty's humour, had some indignant words inscribed, composed by the Revd Edward Massie, the local curate.

Ownership of Gawsworth estate changed in the 1920s. The woods' new owner restored the grave and inscriptions and donated the site to the National Trust.

WHERE SHAKESPEARE'S 'DARK LADY' IS SAID TO WALK

LIME AVENUE AND ST JAMES'S CHURCH, GAWSWORTH

This attractive avenue of lime trees forms a pleasant approach to Gawsworth Hall. Planted in 1827, they and the adjoining church are reputed to be places where the ghost of Mary Fitton – upon whom the 'Dark Lady' of Shakespeare's sonnets is said to be based – walks.

Mary was born in 1578, the daughter of Sir Edward and Lady Alice Fitton of Gawsworth Hall. She became a maid of honour to Elizabeth I in 1596 at the age of 17, but lost this post in 1601 when she became pregnant by William Herbert, the later Earl of Pembroke. After a short spell in the Tower of London, two more illegitimate children followed, after which she married Captain William Polwhele in 1606, only for him to die in 1610. After a further marriage, she died in 1647.

The adjoining St James's Church has its own private access from Gawsworth Hall. Unusually for an Anglican church, it has no aisles. There are a number of tombs of the Fitton family and a small effigy of Mary herself. In the churchyard is the Trooper Memorial, with a slightly unusual inscription. The stone cross in the churchyard in front of the south porch dates from the same time as the church and has carvings of animals representing the expulsion of evil spirits.

Access

In the centre of the village of Gawsworth.

WHERE SPUTNIK WAS FIRST OBSERVED IN THE WEST

LOVELL TELESCOPE, JODRELL BANK

Access

Via Bomish
Lane,
which leads
westwards off
the A535.

Bernard Lovell (who was later knighted) had undertaken valuable work on radar during the Second World War. After the war, when working as a physics lecturer at Manchester University, he was determined to see how radar could be put to use when exploring outer space.

In 1945, he set up an experimental station at Jodrell Bank using ex-army radar equipment. The university already had a botanical research facility here (still represented by the Arboretum), and for Lovell's work it was necessary to choose a locality well away from the electrical interference of a large city.

The first telescope, the Mark 1 (now the Lovell Telescope), was built between 1952 and 1957. Funding for the project was problematical but after its role in tracking the first Soviet satellite (Sputnik 1) had been demonstrated, these problems disappeared. Local mythology tells the tale of a group of five star American Generals approaching the site by rail, when the telescope came into view. One is reputed to have said, 'Just which god-damn end do you look through?'!

The telescope was altered in 1970-71, when it became part of a wider network, called MERLIN, involving smaller satellites in a surrounding network at some distance from Jodrell Bank, but linked by computers. Recently, problems of funding have resurfaced, but it is to be hoped that the future of this magnificent national asset, sometimes irreverently referred to as 'God's Wok', will remain assured.

ONE OF THE OLDEST SURVIVING WOOD AND PLASTER CHURCHES IN EUROPE

CHURCH OF ST JAMES AND ST PAUL, MARTON

This beautiful little half-timbered, black-and-white church was founded in 1343 by Sir John de Davenport and his son, Vivian. Originally called the Chapel of Merton, the oldest part of the church is the nave, the chancel being a later addition.

The bells and tower date from about 1540, and the pulpit from 1620. In 1800, one bell was removed, leaving three, inscribed respectively 'God save the Queene and Realme 1598', 'Jeseus bee our speed 1663' and '1758'.

In 1804, the church roof was lowered and the Minstrel Gallery and dormer windows were removed. The church was restored in 1871 at a cost of £1,500 and a new main entrance was made from the road up the steps and through the belfry. Further restoration took place in 1930-31.

Inside, on the west wall, are traces of medieval paintings.

Access

On the eastern side of the A34, between Alderley Edge and Congleton.

ONCE KNOWN AS THE 'DESERTED VILLAGE'

HAVANNAH VILLAGE, CONGLETON

Access

Via Havannah Lane, which leads off the Congleton–Macclesfield road (A536) just north of the town.

This comparatively isolated community was built to serve the mills that were established here to take advantage of the water power provided by the River Dane. In 1758, Charles Roe, who had introduced silk weaving to Macclesfield, became involved with copper smelting. The year 1763 saw him expanding his operations by leasing land at this location to build a works, which he named Havannah, after the capture of the Cuban capital by the British the previous year. At the same time, some seven cottages were built.

Copper and brass sheets and wire were manufactured here until the early 1800s, when parts of the works were taken over for corn grinding and cotton spinning. More houses were built in about 1826, bringing the total to thirty-nine.

In the late nineteenth century, a tobacco firm started producing genuine Havannah cigars in one of the old silk mills. The venture was clearly successful with the firm moving to larger premises in the town after a few years. The village then became deserted and abandoned, as the factories were not re-occupied. The abandoned village became somewhat of an attraction for visitors to the locality in the early years of the twentieth century.

However, in 1920, a velvet cutting firm moved here from Warrington and the houses were modernised in 1922, when they were provided with water-powered electricity. The velvet cutters left in 1958, but this time, however, the houses were not abandoned. After renovation of the houses in 1976, the place has remained a desirable, if unusual, place to live. At the time of writing, plans for building housing on part of the old mill site were causing some concern locally.

A TOWER SEPARATED FROM ITS CHURCHYARD

ST MARY'S CHURCH, ASTBURY

This church, located on a beautiful site, is a Grade I listed building. It was built in the fifteenth century and is understood to be unchanged from that date. Its detached tower is unusual in the county. The tower, or rather parts of it, dates from the original late Norman church on the site. When the predecessor of the present church was built, it was built further to the south, leaving only a narrow aisle common to the two buildings. When the present building was constructed, it was placed further away still, leaving the present layout.

The first church on this site was a wooden construction, from Anglo-Saxon times, and was noted in the Domesday Book. The first stone church was erected around 1150, and was strengthened about 1240.

In the churchyard is a spectacular hollow yew tree, which has been scientifically dated at over 2,000 years old.

Access

Just off the Congleton–Newcastle road (A34), about a mile south of Congleton.

AN ARISTOCRATIC FOLLY FROM WHERE YOU CAN SEE SEVEN COUNTIES

MOW COP, NEAR SCHOLAR GREEN

Access

Signposted off
the eastern
side of the
A34, south of
Congleton.

This aristocratic folly castle sits exactly on the boundaries of both Cheshire and Staffordshire, between the dioceses of Chester and Lichfield and the provinces of Canterbury and York. It is said that some seven counties can be seen from here.

It was built by Randle Wilbraham of Rode Hall in 1754 to improve the view from his home, to act as a sort of summerhouse, and to provide work for the local unemployed. Some of the masonry was worked by a family from the neighbourhood called Harding.

The high ground at this point, and its location on the borders, encouraged the use of the site by those seeking a place of resort for religious purposes. The Roman Catholics in 1642 were reported as meeting on the hill to hold Mass and for other purposes. It was also used at times as a beacon site.

It was also one of the birthplaces of Primitive Methodism, when Hugh Bourne organised a twelve-hour prayer meeting (also known as a Camp Meeting) here on Sunday, 31 May 1807, with his friend William Clowes. Bourne, a local Methodist preacher, had been enthused by the Camp Meeting movement then popular in the United States, and within a few years Primitive Methodism (often called the 'Ranters') had become a seperate denomination, a status it would retain until most branches of the Methodist Church re-united in the early 1930s.

In 1937, another Camp Meeting was held here. During the meeting, the site's deeds were donated to the National Trust by a local man, Mr Joseph Lovatt, a Wesleyan Methodist who had acquired the site in 1922.

A CANAL MOTORWAY-STYLE 'FLYOVER'

HARDINGS WOOD JUNCTION, NEAR KIDSGROVE

Just north of Kidsgrove, at Hardings Wood, is this motorway-style flyover on the canal system, one of only two on the UK canal system (the other being located a few miles away at Hazelhurst in Staffordshire on the Caldon Canal).

At this point, the Trent & Mersey Canal (completed in 1777) travels in a roughly east-west direction. Travelling westwards, the canal's 'Hall Green Branch' leaves the 'main line' on the left-hand side, just like a motorway slip road, and then travels parallel to the 'main line' whilst maintaining its level. The 'main line' in the meantime drops its level by way of two locks, after which the Hall Green Branch then crosses the 'main line' by way of the Red Bull Aqueduct, as shown in the photograph. The Hall Green Branch then runs in a northerly direction and connects with the Macclesfield Canal (completed in 1831) at Hall Green, about half a mile distant. (Guidebooks often refer to the Macclesfield Canal starting at the junction with the 'main line'.)

Some early nineteenth-century 'canal politics' were at work here. When the Macclesfield Canal obtained their Authorising Act in 1827 (effectively a form of 'compulsory purchase order), the older Trent & Mersey Canal obtained a similar Act, allowing them to build the first one and half miles of the new canal as far as Hall Green.

Access

From the towpath of either canal.

A MUSEUM COMMEMORATING PRIMITIVE METHODISM

ENGLESEA BROOK CHAPEL

Access

Located to the south west of Barthomley, on Englesea Brook Lane.

This little chapel, set in a very pleasant location, is now part of a museum devoted to the establishment of Primitive Methodism, a revivalist faction of Methodism that emerged after 1807, involving populist methods of worship such as the Camp Meeting held at Mow Cop that year.

Built in 1828 to a simple square design, the chapel has close association with the origin of Primitive Methodism. One of its founders, Hugh Bourne, is buried in the churchyard on the other side of the road.

The adjoining Sunday school building, built in 1914 to the memory of Hugh Bourne, comprises a museum containing pottery, banners and other memorabilia of the movement.

The chapel itself was provided with a balcony in 1832 to provide fifty extra seats by means of box pews. A small pipe organ, with very narrow pipes, dates from 1828 and can be heard on occasions. A magic lantern show from 1907 and a film made in 1948 at Mow Cop can also be seen.

THE SYMBOLS OF SANDBACH

SAXON CROSSES, SANDBACH

These two crosses are symbolic of Sandbach and date from the eighth or ninth centuries AD, and are believed to commemorate the arrival of Christianity in central England around AD 653. They are large in scale, at over 16ft and 10ft 9in respectively, much larger than most of their contemporaries. What stands today are only the shafts of the crosses.

Current thinking is that the crosses marked the presence of an important Saxon church or monastery at Sandbach, around which there were some three crosses. The two largest ones were moved to the town's market place at some time in the late Middle Ages or shortly after, as they are mentioned in 1565. Their engravings tell the story of Christ and the Mercian King Penda's son, Peada, who became a Christian.

A later description of the town from 1621 does not mention them and it is possible that they were destroyed by the Puritans either in 1613 or later during the Civil War. Some of the stones were then used in local buildings in the town, but the two main inscribed fragments were removed by Sir John Crewe to his estates at Utkinton after 1670, thence to Tarporley rectory, and finally to Oulton Park, where they were built into a grotto.

These pieces were returned to the town in 1816 after a combined effort by Sir John Egerton of Oulton, John Palmer and George Ormerod. The two crosses seen today are a combination of the carved main pieces, other sections recovered from elsewhere in the town, and plain pieces of stone to replace missing sections. In Sandbach churchyard are some further fragments, placed there in the 1950s, and thought to be from the third, and smallest, cross.

Access
In the centre of Market Place.

THE SHORTEST CANAL IN ENGLAND

WARDLE CANAL, MIDDLEWICH

Access

Off Lewin
Street (A533)
to the south
of the town
centre, near to
the junction
with Brooks
Lane.

At 154ft in length, including the first lock, this is said to be the shortest canal in England. Most, however, will not regard it as a separate canal at all, but as part of the Middlewich branch of the Shropshire Union Canal. Strictly speaking, it is the Wardle (or Wardle Green) Branch of the Trent & Mersey Canal, even though the village of Wardle is many miles away, at the other end of the Middlewich branch.

It also had its origins in the 'canal politics' of the early nineteenth century. The Trent & Mersey Canal had been the only route from the Midlands to the North West and Merseyside. However, the construction of the Shropshire Union Canal, authorised in 1825, threatened the business of the Trent & Mersey by offering a straighter and therefore quicker route. When the new company sought parliamentary approval to build a branch from Barbridge to Middlewich, they were allowed to build it no closer than 100 yards of the older Trent & Mersey Canal, i.e. they could not make a connection between the two.

The Trent and Mersey were, however, allowed to make the connection in the form of the Wardle Canal, which opened on 1 September 1833 at a cost of £129,000. They were also allowed to charge extortionate 'compensation tolls', amounting to 9*d* a ton for travelling the short canal. This state of affairs persisted until the 1880s.

The Wardle Canal, as well as being the shortest canal in England, was also the most expensive to use!

TO REMIND CHILDREN OF THE IMPORTANCE OF TIME

VILLAGE HALL, CREWE GREEN

The village of Crewe Green lies a few miles east of Crewe. Confusingly, until 1974, when the 'Green' was added, it was just called Crewe.

There is not much of a village here, although recent proposals by the Duchy of Lancaster – which owns around 4,000 acres in the area – to create a 'Poundbury' style village, have caused controversy.

Crewe Green's current village hall started life as the village school and was built in Victorian days. Built no doubt with some aristocratic benefaction, the building itself was clearly designed to impress its young inmates with clear ideas of the value of time.

Access

On the northern side of the B5077, to the east of Crewe.

The frontage contains a sundial and a carved panel, with the inscriptions 'Use well thy time', 'What shall we render unto the Lord' and 'Time rewarding Industry and Punishing Sloth'. The panel has a winged effigy of Time, holding in one hand a whip, used to threaten a lazy boy clothed in rag and lying amongst weeds by a ruinous home, and in the other hand a laurel wreath, being presented to an industrious lad holding a spade.

AN OCTAGONAL CHURCH TOWER, 'JACK IN THE GREEN' AND A CARVING OF THE DEVIL

ST MARY'S CHURCH, NANTWICH

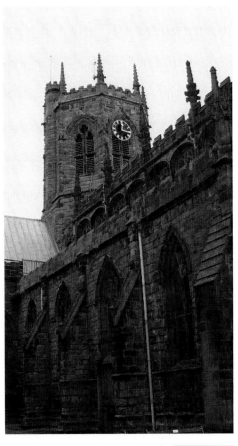

This is Nantwich's most ancient building, and is often referred to as the 'Cathedral of South Cheshire'. Built largely in the fourteenth century, it is the focal point of the town centre, and is built of red sandstone. Its tower is octagonal in construction.

Internally, the most notable features are the twenty ornate canopied choir stalls, or miserichords. Another internal feature in the north transept is 'Jack the Green' or 'the Green Man', the pagan fertility god who lived in an oak tree. Why he is here is not clear – it could be because the church was built on the site of a wood, and this was some form of joking appeasement to him.

Outside, at the junction of the nave and the north transept, is a gargoyle showing a devil of exceptional depravity bearing off with a woman's pitcher. It is said that the masons employed on the church at the time had returned to their lodgings one night, only to find their landlady helping herself to their money which they kept in a pitcher. They then took it upon themselves to immortalise her in stone.

St Mary's is one of the few buildings that was not destroyed in Nantwich's Great Fire of 1583, which lasted for twenty days and destroyed most of the town. Queen Elizabeth I, knowing the value of the town to the salt industry, donated £1,000 towards the town's rebuilding. Thomas Cleese, a local builder, expressed his gratitude on the front of his house in the main square, now called the 'Queen's Aid House', by inscribing the following words on the upper floor of the building:

Access

In the centre of the town, on Churchyard Side.

God grant our ryal Queen
In England long to raign
For she hath put her helping hand
To bild this towne again.

FROM WIDOWS ALMSHOUSES TO THE CHESHIRE CAT

'CURSHAW'S AT THE CAT', NANTWICH

Access

On Welsh Row, just outside the town centre.

This building started life as six cottages early in the seventeenth century. In 1676, they were converted by local landowner, Sir Roger Wilbraham, into three almshouses in commemoration of the death of his wife and two sons, who all died on the same day.

They became known as the Widow's or Wilbraham Almshouses. Two women were meant to share each cottage, with a dividing line allocating equal shares, though it is understood that disagreements were common! During the nineteenth century, six new cottages were added at the rear.

By 1945, the almshouses were derelict. This prompted local businessman, William Scholfield, to buy and restore them over the next six years. The result was the well known 'Cheshire Cat' licenced restaurant, which later became a licenced club and is now 'Curshaw's'. An old mounting block can be seen on the street outside.

Sir Roger Wilbraham also built six almshouses for poor men. These are situated further out of town at nos 112-116 Welsh Row. They were rebuilt in 1870 on an adjoining site and are now referred to as the Tollemache Almshouses.

A FINE EXAMPLE OF AN ELIZABETHAN MERCHANT'S HOUSE

CHURCHE'S MANSION, NANTWICH

This is a fine example of an Elizabethan half-timbered merchant's house. It was built for the merchant Richard Churche and his wife, Margerye, in 1577, by Thomas Clease. At the time of its construction, it was on the edge of the town and so escaped destruction in the Great Fire of 1583.

The entrance porch contains carved portraits of Richard and Margerye, and on the front there are various emblems, including a lion, salamander and an ape.

In 1930, the building was threatened with being transported to the United States, but fortunately was rescued and restored by Edgar Myott. For many years, it served as a restaurant and museum and most recently as an antique shop.

Nantwich is well worth further exploration, with many historical buildings. In the Cocoa House Yard is the Millennium Clock, designed and built by Welsh clock maker and artist Paul Beckett. Next to it is a chimney, formerly part of a wheelwrights forge making parts for the adjoining Welch's Coach Manufactury.

On Beam Street are the Wright, Crewe and Hope Almshouses. The Wright Almshouses were originally built on London Road in 1638, but were moved here stone by stone to stand next to the Crewe Almshouses at a later date.

Access

At the roundabout at the eastern end of Hospital Street.

A MEMORIAL TO A BRAVE MAN WHO AVOIDED NEEDLESS CASUALTIES

ARTHUR BROWN MEMORIAL, NANTWICH

Access

Via a footpath which runs along the eastern side of the River Weaver, accessible from Shrewbridge Road, on the south-western side of the town.

This touching memorial commemorates Lt Arthur L. Brown, who crashed his US Army Air Force P47 Thunderbolt near Nantwich on 14 January 1944, and was killed. Eyewitness reports at the time say that he steered the stricken plane away from the centre of Nantwich, thereby avoiding civilian casualties. The aircraft finally nose-dived into some quicksand near the River Weaver. Lt Brown was only 23 at the time.

His selfless action, like a number of other similar occurances during the Second World War, earned him a lot of local respect. A local ironmonger, who owned the field leading to the crash site, erected a memorial in the form of a makeshift grave. This was attended to by a local Brownie pack, who adorned the 'grave' with flowers. In 1985, responsibility for the site was assumed by the local branch of the Cheshire Regiment Association.

Shortly afterwards, the stone was replaced by a local stonemason free of charge, and various other people lent a hand. The new memorial was dedicated in a service attended by Lt Brown's sister from New York, and was conducted by a local clergyman, formerly a wartime RAF pilot. Wreaths continue to be laid here every Remembrance Sunday.

ONCE A SECRET GOVERNMENT NUCLEAR BUNKER

HACK GREEN SECRET NUCLEAR BUNKER

This site was first used for military purposes during the Second World War, when it was a 'Starfish' site where a mock town was constructed out of lighting arrays to confuse enemy night bombers looking for the vital railway junction at Crewe. A number of such sites were built at various locations in the UK. A GCI (Ground Control Interception) radar facility was also added.

Following the Cherry Report of 1949, a number of radar sites, including Hack Green, were upgraded in the early 1950s as part of the ROTOR project, to meet the increased threat of nuclear attack by the Soviet Union. Those on the western side of the country were provided with semi-submerged concrete 'R6' blockhouses with walls some 10ft thick.

Access
Just off the Whitchurch Road (A530), a few miles south of Nantwich.

ROTOR soon became outdated by technological advances. After a spell as an Air Traffic Control facility, Hack Green was abandoned in 1966. In the early 1980s, however, following a heightening of the Cold War, the centre was re-activated and modernised as a Regional Government Headquarters, one of seventeen in the country. It retained this status until declared surplus by the government in 1992. It later opened to the public as a museum with a Cold War theme.

Around 130 civil servants and military commanders would have lived here in the event of such a war. Its last use has been well preserved, complete with early 1980s computer technology. There are communications centres, a BBC studio, a fallout centre and decontamination rooms split over three floors. The 1960s 'banned' BBC film *The War Game* can also be seen here.

At one end is an internal stairwell extending the full height of the structure. Because it was feared that some of the inmates might wish to jump and commit suicide in the event of living in such a confined space for months on end, the stairwell was (and is) decorated in an 'optimistic' lemon yellow colour!

A GRAVESTONE COMMEMORATING A CRICKETING LEGEND

ALBERT HORNBY GRAVESTONE, ACTON

This interesting gravestone commemorates Albert Neilson Hornby, the sixth son of William Henry Hornby, a cotton mill proprietor and director of the Lancashire & Yorkshire Railway who was Member of Parliament for Blackburn from 1857 to 1865. Hornby came from a sporting family, lived most of his life at Church Minshull, and is buried here at Acton.

Having played cricket for his school in 1867, he was playing for the Lancashire County Cricket Club by 1870. A Tory county councillor, he was known as the 'cricketing squire'.

He played rugby and cricket for England, and was the first man to captain England in both sports. In 1877 he played for the MCC in their centennial match against England. The year 1882 saw him captaining England in the Test match against Australia at the Oval, when the Ashes were lost. He was President of the Lancashire club for twenty years.

Described as 'a little man with neat features, a short military moustache, and his hair parted in the middle', he earned the nickname 'Monkey'. He played his last match in 1899 and died in December 1925, aged 78. His signature is carved on the gravestone.

Access

Acton churchyard, on the side closest to the main Chester Road (A534).

A RATHER LARGE VILLAGE LOCK-UP

THE ROUND HOUSE, CHORLEY

This octagonal building, now a listed building, was originally the village 'lock-up' for the area, being built in the eighteenth century. Indeed, the 'Round House' was one of the terms used for describing village lock-ups or bridewells. Its large size is rather unusual in such an isolated and sparsely populated area.

The building is now a normal dwelling house, and all its rooms radiate from the centre.

Access

On the south side of Nantwich Road, near the memorial garden.

HOW A POACHER EXTRACTED REVENGE ON HIS PROSECUTORS

IMAGE HOUSE, BUNBURY

Access

On the western side of the A49, just south of its junction with Betty's Lane.

This little cottage, built in the early nineteenth century, is noted for the curious carved heads and reliefs incorporated around the front door and at the first floor level. It is said that they are the work of the builder of the house, a local poacher, who had been transported abroad for his misdemeanors. When he returned home, he built the house and adorned its frontage with the likenesses of the gamekeepers, law and justice officials who had been involved in his punishment. He was determined to extract some form of revenge on them, though whether this involved witchcraft or other powers, as has been suggested, is not known.

The Image House has another story to it – namely that it was built 'in a single night between sunset and sunrise'. If it was built on 'common land', the builder could claim a right of residence, so long as the chimney was seen to be in use by dawn, following which the rest of the house could be completed in due course. Although never a strictly legal right, it seems to have been a right acquired by custom and practice at the time.

Beatrice Tunstall, in her novel *The Shiny Night*, published in 1931, names the poacher as Seth Stone.

THIS MAN COMMANDED A SHIP AT THE AGE OF 88

SIR GEORGE BEESTON'S TOMB, ST BONIFACE'S CHURCH, BUNBURY

Within the sanctuary of this beautiful and historic church is the tomb of Sir George Beeston. He was Admiral of the Fleet in Tudor times and served under four monarchs. At the age of 88 (some say 89) he commanded the ship *Dreadnought* when it fought against the Spanish Armada in 1588, breaking the Spanish line along with four other ships. He was knighted for his services and lived on to the grand age of 102. The tomb contains an elaborate painted front, which was restored to its original colours in 1937.

Sir George was a descendant of Sir Hugh Calveley, whose elaborate alabaster tomb or memorial, said to be the oldest such tomb in Cheshire, can be seen elsewhere in the church. He was a famous warrior who died in 1385, whose generous endowments led to the creation of the church we see at Bunbury today.

Also worth seeing, in the south aisle of the church, are painted screens dating back to the fifteenth century. These were restored by the Victoria and Albert Museum in 1988.

Access

St Boniface's Church is situated in the centre of the village.

WHERE THE FASHIONABLE ONCE CAME FOR A CURE

SPURSTOW SPA, SPURSTOW

This small spring is marked on the Ordnance Survey map as being saline, but judging by its taste today, this is not the case. Nor was it the case in 1819 when Ormerod did his great survey of the county, when he identified it as containing mainly sulphates of Sodium and Magnesium. It was also known as Spurstow White Water.

It is claimed that the spa had been found by accident and that it was curative for skin disorders. The bath house (now Bath House Farm, to the north of the spa) was built in the sixteenth century. Those attending the spa would also meet in the dining room of the bath house and hold 'Healing Services'.

Samuel Lewis's *Topographical Directory of England* in 1848 describes the spa as 'formerly much frequented and a bath house was erected by Sir Thomas Mostyn for the accommodation of visitors, but that the waters are not at present in repute.'

As late as 1930, a sign could be seen by the Crewe Arms, stating, 'If you are troubled with sore or flow, this is the way to Spurstow Spa'.

Today, apart from the farm buildings, the spa is just a couple of stone troughs set in an almost forgotten woodland.

Access

Strictly speaking this 'curiosity' is inaccessible, being on private land. However, public footpaths run nearby. The best access is via the footpath that leads from Capper Lane opposite Pear Tree Farm. At the end of the marked path, cross the field diagonally (respecting farming operations) walking towards the near edge of Spurstow Plantation, where a footpath leads through. At the other edge of the wood, turn left onto another footpath, following the wood's edge. The spa itself is in the wood to the left after a couple of minute's walk.

WHERE THE DOG WHIPPER USED TO SIT

DOG WHIPPER'S PEW, ST MARGARET'S CHURCH, WRENBURY

This church is full of boxed pews, each with their own door. Right by the main entrance, marked with a small metal plaque, is the 'Dog Whipper's Pew', said to date from about 1734.

    The job of the Dog Whipper was to remove unruly dogs from the service, but his more frequent duty was to keep members of the congregation awake in the days when the priest's sermons might last an hour or two. He was paid ten shillings a year for his duties, and was given a blue gown with a yellow tippet.

    The title of the post changed to Beadle in 1826. Its last holder, Thomas Vaughan, died in 1879.

Access

On the north side of Nantwich Road, in the centre of the village.

CHESHIRE'S OWN LEANING TOWER

FORMER ST CHAD'S CHURCH TOWER, WYBUNBURY

This tower is Cheshire's equivalent of Italy's Leaning Tower of Pisa. Together with the now-demolished St Chad's Church, it was built in the late fifteenth century. Like the Leaning Tower, it was built on 'bad ground' which could not support the weight of the structure, in this case through the action of underground springs.

The church was substantially altered in 1595 and 1790, but by 1750, it was noticed that the tower had begun to lean to the north east. Eighty years later, the top of the tower was nearly 6ft from true vertical, and so, in 1834, the main church structure was rebuilt by the contractor James Trubshaw. Whilst doing this work, he dug sufficient clay from beneath some of the old foundations to make the tower regain the vertical.

His solution did not work in the longer term and the church was again taken down and rebuilt in 1893. Earlier in the twentieth century, the chancel was taken down and recreated within the nave, but even this did not succeed. The church, minus tower, was finally demolished in 1976 and a new building erected a quarter of a mile to the north.

By now, the tower was some 4ft from true vertical, and considered unsafe. A Nottingham-based engineering company, which had carried out work on the Leaning Tower of Pisa, were engaged to install new foundations whilst the tower was held on over 100 hydraulic jacks. This work was finished in 1989.

The tower is now safe and protected from any threat of future leaning. However, like its Italian counterpart, it has been left with a definite slant, in this case between 18in and 2ft, so it can continue to be called the Leaning Church Tower of Wybunbury.

Access

Off Bridge Street (B5071) at the eastern end of the village.

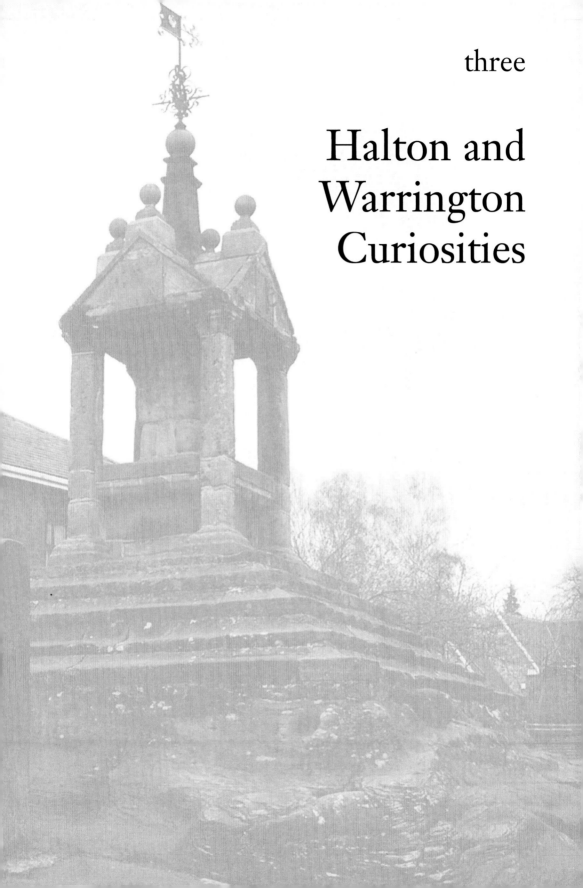

three

Halton and Warrington Curiosities

THE BURIAL PLACE OF THE 'CHILDE OF HALE'

JOHN MIDDLETON'S GRAVE, HALE

Access

In the churchyard on Church Road.

This part of Cheshire, which, until 1974, was part of Lancashire, has a definite Merseyside accent to it.

It is the birthplace and burial place of one of England's tallest men, John Middleton, the 'Childe of Hale'. Born in 1578 into a poor family, he had grown to some 9ft 3in tall by the time he was 20. He was taken into the employment of Sir Gilbert Ireland, the local Lord of the Manor, who used him as a bodyguard. When Sir Gilbert was called to visit the court of King James I in 1617, he took John with him.

Shortly after, John was invited to wrestle with the King's champion, and easily but gracefully beat the man. The King took this well, but then sent John home with £20; at the time a considerable sum. On their way back, they called at Sir Gilbert's old Oxford college, Brazennose, and John is reputed to have left an imprint of his hand on one of the college's walls. Sometime after 1815, the college's rowing club named their rowing eights boat after him, which is still the case today. They also wear his colours of purple, yellow and red. The college also has one life-sized painting, two smaller portraits and two life-sized representations of John's hands. Another portrait, that of John in his 'London clothes', hangs in Liverpool's Speke Hall.

His fortunes suffered on the rest of his journey when he was robbed and he was obliged to 'follow the plough to his dying day', which occurred in 1623. His nickname – the 'Childe of Hale' – arises from the fact that although he was tall and powerful, he was a gentle giant. The thatched cottage where he lived in the village can still be seen, and is not far from the local pub, which is named after him.

THE LAST REMAINING DUCK DECOY IN THE NORTH WEST

HALE DUCK DECOY

This is the only surviving duck decoy in North West England. It is a scheduled Ancient Monument.

The decoy is surrounded by a 5 metre-wide moat laid out in a pentagon shape, crossed by a small bridge. A continuous clay bank surrounds the moat as a protection against high tides, as the decoy is close to the Mersey. Within the centre of the decoy is a freshwater pond, with curving arms, known as decoy pipes, each about 20 metres long, that end in small areas of woodland. Each pipe would have been covered by hoops made of hazel or willow (iron was used later), that diminished in size towards the pipe's end that would have been covered with netting.

The ducks were caught for food or for onward sale. When in operation, the decoy man would approach the pipes from an upwind direction, and with the aid of a small dog, the ducks would be led to the narrow end of the pipe, where they would then be caught after being 'flushed down' by the decoy man.

The decoy was built in the seventeenth century by the owner of the nearby Hale Hall, probably Sir Gilbert Ireland. A date of 1633 has been found on a stone found on the site. In 1754, various improvements were undertaken. There is a small brick building on the site for use by the decoy man.

Duck decoys fell out of use towards the end of the nineteenth century and this one was last used around 1920. From the 1960s, interest in its restoration began to grow, and a lease of the site was taken by the local authorities. In recent years, ditches and pipes have been cleared out, hoops restored and new screens installed. A new bridge has been erected, and the decoy man's cottage was rebuilt between 1976 and 1982.

Access

From the centre of Widnes via Dutton Lane, Hale Gate Road and Mersey View Road. There is no public access to the site other than by the occasional guided tours, which start from the Visitor Centre at Pickerings Pasture Nature Reserve.

ONCE KNOWN AS THE 'SAILOR'S CHURCH'

CHRIST CHURCH, WESTON POINT

Access

This cannot be approached directly without seeking permission to enter the port grounds, which, at the time of writing, is in the throes of redevelopment. From the Weston Point Expressway (A557), travel via Sandy Lane, South Road and West Road to reach the dock gates.

This Grade II listed building is built in local sandstone in an Early English style. It was provided in 1841 by the Trustees of the Weaver Navigation Company for their employees and families. Its architect was Edmund Sharpe of Lancaster.

Originally, it stood on a headland at the side of the River Mersey, but when the Manchester Ship Canal was built in the 1890s, it finished up being on a sort of island. A claim was made at the time that it was the only church in Britain to be built on an uninhabited island. It was a chapel of ease originally to All Saints' Church in Runcorn, and from 1930 to the Church of St John the Evangelist in Weston.

It ceased to be used for services at the end of 1991 and was declared redundant in 1995. In 2004, planning permission was granted for it to be used as offices, storage and as a monument, but at the time of being photographed it was semi-derelict, and its stonework in need of some cleaning. Its future will inevitably be tied in with the redevelopment of the dockland area.

A CASTLE THAT DESERVES TO BE BETTER KNOWN

HALTON CASTLE, RUNCORN

Halton Castle is one of the lesser-known castles of England. Situated amongst the housing estates of Runcorn, it is open to the public on only a few occasions each year.

Construction work is thought to have commenced around 1071 by Hugh Lupus, Earl of Chester (sometimes called Hugh D'Avranches), who had been awarded the county by William the Conqueror in return for help in the Norman Conquest. He in turn bestowed it upon his nephew, Nigel. Originally it would have been a motte and bailey structure. The current stone structure would have been started in the latter half of the twelfth century, and was added to over the years.

The castle was used as a minor administrative centre, court, prison and depository for court records. In the Civil War, it was held for the Crown, but fell to the Parliamentarians in 1643 and the following year. Some dismantling took place after the war on the orders of Cromwell. A courthouse (now the Castle Hotel) was built in 1738 with some of the stonework from the gate towers.

After the 1660 Restoration, its ownership reverted to the Crown, but in 2002 the local authority and the Norton Priory Museum Trust were entrusted with management of the castle with the aim of making it more accessible.

A couple of hundred yards down Castle Road, is another fascinating building, Sir John Chesshyre's Library. Built in 1730 at Sir John's expense, he provided it with a stock of 500 or so volumes of theological books for the free use of 'divines of the Church of England, or other gentlemen or persons of letters'. Effectively, this was a free public library, although it was only open on Tuesdays. It no longer serves this purpose and is now part of the parish hall of St Mary's Church.

Access

Via Halton Brow and Main Street, in the Castlefields area.

A REMINDER TO A FAMOUS CHILDREN'S AUTHOR

LEWIS CARROLL'S BIRTHPLACE, DARESBURY

This metal plaque, set in a neat enclosure in the midst of open countryside, is all that remains to mark the birthplace of Lewis Carroll, born Charles Lutwidge Dodgson, the author of well-known children's classics such as *Alice Through the Looking Glass*, *The Hunting of the Snark* and *Jaberwocky*.

Dodgson was born here on 27 January 1832, at what was then Daresbury Parsonage, the third of eleven children. As well as being a noted children's author, he was also a mathematician, logician, an Anglican deacon, and a photographer. His facility at word play, logic and fantasy has delighted audiences ranging from children to the literary elite, and beyond this his work has become embedded deeply in modern culture, directly influencing many artists. He died on 14 January 1898.

The parsonage itself, about one and a half miles away from the church it served, burnt down in 1883, and the bricks and slates were then used in nearby farm buildings. The site has recently been taken over by the National Trust, who are undertaking a series of improvements. A memorial window in Daresbury church shows characters from *Alice's Adventures in Wonderland*.

Lewis Carroll's reminiscences of his early life were set out in the collection of poems known as *Three Sunsets and Other Poems*, published in 1898:

An island farm mid seas of corn
Sawyed by the wandering breath of morn
This happy spot where I was born.

Access

At the junction of Morphany Lane and Higher Lane – a footpath leads to the site.

ONE OF ONLY THREE TRANSPORTER BRIDGES REMAINING IN THE UK

CROSFIELDS TRANSPORTER BRIDGE, WARRINGTON

This steel bridge, sometimes called the Bank Quay Transporter Bridge, crosses the River Mersey, with a span of 200ft. Such bridges, with their distinctive travelling car or platform, were usually built where it was necessary to retain the rights of navigation on a river, as was the case here. It is 30ft wide and 76ft above the normal water level, and has an overall length of 339ft. The control cabin is located at the top of the one of the supporting towers.

It was built in 1913-16 at a cost of £35,000, replacing an earlier bridge from 1908 that had cost £4,000. Designed by William Henry Hunter, it was built by William Arrol & Co. Ltd, bridge and crane builders of Glasgow, and its completion was delayed by the First World War.

The bridge was not a public bridge, and was provided to link the parts of Joseph Crosfield's soap and chemicals factory on the north side of the river with his cement works on the south side. Originally designed to carry rail vehicles of up to 18 tons, it was converted to carry road traffic in 1940 and in 1953 was modified to carry increased loads of up to 30 tons.

It was taken out of use in 1963-4 when a new road bridge with a lower height clearance was built, linking the two sites, river traffic having ceased many years previously. For a few years, the transporter bridge was maintained in operative condition, and saw occasional use up to the early 1970s.

After the firm threatened to demolish it, it was declared a listed building in 1976 and is now an Ancient Monument. Some public money was spent undertaking immediate repairs and repainting it, and eventually the local authority took it over on a fifty-year lease. However, it is currently in a poor condition.

A similar bridge still operates in Middlesbrough, one is currently out of use in Newport, South Wales, and one (now demolished) operated in nearby Runcorn up to 1961.

Access

This bridge is quite hard to find, and close vehicular access is not possible. Take the unclassified road off the south side of Wilson Patten Street, signposted to the Warrington Speedkarting Centre. Park opposite the Cats Protection League buildings and the bridge will soon come into view. A footpath leads to the riverbank, which it is possible to walk along towards the bridge.

THE FINEST DECORATED GATES IN THE COUNTRY

GATES TO BANK HALL, WARRINGTON

Access

At the junction of Sankey Street and Appley Street, in the town centre.

These gates are said to be among the finest in the country. They were originally made and exhibited in 1862 by the Coalbrookdale Company for the International Exhibition, held in London that year. They were designed by a Mr Kershaw.

The original design for the gates had the Prince of Wales feathers, a wreath and the German motto '*Ich Dien*', meaning 'I Serve', in the centre. It seems that the gates had actually been ordered by one of the London Livery companies as a gift to Queen Victoria, to be used at Sandringham after the Great Exhibition in 1851. Prior to delivery, they were to be inspected by the Queen and were erected in Rotten Row, in front of a statue of Oliver Cromwell by the same designer. This caused the Queen displeasure, and as a result, the gates never made it to Sandringham.

Instead, they went back to Coalbrookdale. They were seen there in 1893 by a Mr Frederick Monks, a member of the Council and a director of the Monks Hall Foundry at Coalbrookdale. He bought them and presented them as a gift to the Council, being formally opened on Walking Day* 1895. They are now surmounted by what were the Borough's arms from 1847 to 1897. To celebrate the Queen's Silver Jubilee in 1978, they were painted in the resplendant gold leaf that remains today.

The infamous statue of Cromwell also made it to Warrington, where it now resides at Bridge Foot. Whenever Her Majesty the Queen visits the town, her route is always designed to avoid passing the statue!

* Walking Day is a Warrington tradition dating from 1832, and is held on the Friday nearest to 1 July. It is a procession of Christian witness and its route always starts through these gates.

IS THIS THE ORIGINAL CHESHIRE CAT?

ST WILFRIDS' CHURCH, GRAPPENHALL

A church has stood in Grappenhall since 1120, although the present building dates from about 400 years later. The tower itself dates from 1539. The church is in one of the most beautiful locations in the whole of the county.

On the west wall of the tower, at a considerable height on one of the string courses of stonework, is this grinning cat. It is claimed to be the inspiration for the Cheshire Cat in Lewis Carroll's *Alice's Adventures in Wonderland*.

The reason for its carving is not known. It could have been a pun in the name Caterall, believed to have been one of the church's builders or masons. Alternatively, it could be a pun on Caterich, a property owned by the local Boydell family.

On the south side of the village, amongst the new housing estates, is a walled garden known as Grappenhall Heys. Originally, this was the site of a house of the same name built by the Parr family, who ran Parr's Bank, which subsequently became part of the National Westminster Bank. The garden opened to the public in 2002, and is worth a brief visit.

Access

From the A50 on the edge of Warrington via Bellhouse Lane and Church Lane.

A TREE DESCENDED FROM THE GLASTONBURY THORN

APPLETON THORN

This attractive tree was grown from a cutting taken from the Glastonbury Thorn at Glastonbury Abbey, the tree that is reputed to have sprouted from the staff of Joseph of Arimathea after he returned to the area to visit his mines following the death of Christ.

The current tree dates from October 1967, and is looked after by the local Women's Institute. However, a similar tree has stood on this site since 1178, when local knight and landowner, Adam de Dutton, returning from the Crusades via Glastonbury, planted one.

A tree was still on the site in 1880, when it was removed to Arley Park, and replaced with another planted by Mrs Piers Egerton-Warburton, to commemorate her marriage. Her father-in-law, Rowland Egerton-Warburton, celebrated the event by writing one of his witty songs.

High winds in 1965 blew down this tree. It successor was short-lived and was replaced by the current tree two years later.

One of England's traditional rural ceremonies, which dates from the Middle Ages, has been that of 'bawming the thorn', 'bawming' being another word for 'adorning'. In this, the tree is adorned with red ribbons and fresh flowers, after which dancing takes place around it in a circle.

At Appleton, the ceremony appears to have started in Victorian times, but died out some time after 1891, when Rowland died, as it had started to attract raucous crowds from nearby Warrington. After another temporary revival that ended in the 1930s, it was reinstated in 1967 and occurs around the third Sunday in June involving children from Appleton Thorn Primary School.

Access

At the junction of Stretton Road (B5356) with Lumb Brook Lane, just opposite the church.

A REMINDER OF A CITY THAT NEVER WAS

INSCRIPTION ON PICKERING ARMS, THELWALL

This pub contains a commemoration of the founding of a 'city' that almost certainly never took place. On the side of the building below the roof are the words, 'In the year 923 King Edward the Elder founded a city here and called it Thelwall'.

The Anglo-Saxon Chronicle says: 'In this year went King Edward with a force, after harvest, and bade build the city and occupy and man it'.

What the statements refer to are a brief stage in the struggle in which Edward was trying to recapture the northern part of Danelaw from the Viking Ragnald. He was actually referring to the construction of a 'burh', or a fortified stronghold of earth and timber, to be occupied by local troops and paid for by the locality. His aim would have been to protect the crossing point of the Mersey at Warrington. It is thought that this would have taken place in around 919-20 rather than 923.

Certainly, there is no evidence that a city was ever built, though the trappings of modern urbanised life all too apparent nowadays with the noise of traffic from the nearby infamous motorway viaduct.

Access

On the south side of the main road through the village (B5157).

THE ONLY GRADE I LISTED STRUCTURE IN THE WARRINGTON AREA

LYMM CROSS

Access

In the centre of Lymm, via the A6144.

This sandstone cross is the only Grade I listed structure in the Warrington area. It is not known exactly when it was built – both the fourteenth and seventeenth centuries have been suggested. The architects, Paley and Austin, were responsible for its restoration in 1897 to commemorate Queen Victoria's Diamond Jubilee.

The shaft of the cross stands on the roof of a square pavilion with square pillars at each corner. A stone ball and weather vane stand above the cross itself. On three of the sides are bronze sundials from 1897 with the words, 'We are a Shadow', 'Save Time' and 'Think of the Last'. Also at that time, the worn steps were re-faced and a symbolic golden crown replaced an old cockerel on the weather vane.

Why the cross was built is not known. Lymm has never had a market, so it is certainly not a market cross. It could have replaced an earlier Saxon or even a Roman structure. One theory is that the stone base, carved into steps from a natural rock outlier, had at one time contained a statue of the Roman goddess, Minerva.

Local people, however, are proud of their cross and it is certainly symbolic of Lymm. After serious damage by vandals in 2005, it was quickly repaired. The village stocks stand close by.

THE SOLE REMINDER OF A GARDEN VILLAGE THAT WAS NEVER BUILT

CROSSFIELD BRIDGE, LYMM

This bridge, and the roads that lead to it are the sole reminders of a possible garden village that would have been built in the area by William Hesketh Lever, of Sunlight Soap and Port Sunlight fame.

Lever bought the Beechwood Estate, which included Lymm Dam, at the beginning of the twentieth century from George Dewhurst. It is thought that Lever had in mind an excursion into the Cheshire salt industry, Lymm then having a small number of salt works. This village would have housed his workers at any factories he set up in the area and would have been a garden village, in similar style to, but smaller in scale than, Port Sunlight. However, in venturing into salt, he would have attracted the opposition of the existing salt producers. In the end he might have reached an 'understanding' with them to keep out of salt if they kept out of soap.

All that happened with Lever's plans for the village was the building of the roads currently known as Lakeside Road, The Avenue and the bridleway running along the eastern side of the dam, plus this bridge, constructed just after the First World War by local contractor, Harry Fairclough. The roads were planted with English elm and Lombardy poplars, although the former succumbed to Dutch elm disease in the 1980s.

Lever himself died in 1925 and Beechwood was demolished in the 1930s. The estate was then divided and the dam came into local authority ownership, which remains to this day. The bridge itself has never been required to carry any substantial traffic.

Access

At the upper end of Lymm Dam, near the junctions of Lakeside Road and The Avenue.

INDEX

Other local titles published by The History Press

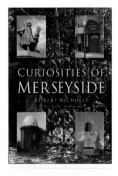

Curiosities of Merseyside

ROBERT NICHOLLS

Whether it be unusual buildings, natural features or just places associated with a fascinating story, these pages reveal an area abounding in interest. See *Titanic*-related memorials, Britain's largest cathedral organ, a series of tunnels that lead nowhere, lighthouses built inland, the back-to-front Town Hall, and the 'Puzzle Stones', as well as more recent reminders of the areas contributions to the world of sport and popular music. Over 150 Curiosities of Merseyside can be found within these pages.

978 0 7509 3984 3

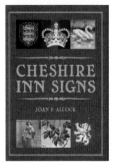

Cheshire Inn Signs

JOAN P. ALCOCK

This charming book takes the reader on a tour of Cheshire's inns past and present, discovering the origins of names such as the Bleeding Wolf, the Swan With Two Necks and the Wizard of Edge. Illustrated with over 100 images, *Cheshire Inn Signs* lists the huge variety of signs found around the county and offers a fascinating insight into the history of these highly crafted items. It will delight all those interested in the story behind the signs, as well as proving to be a valuable guide for those who wish to locate them around the county.

978 0 7524 4770 4

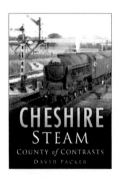

Cheshire Steam: County of Contrasts

DAVID PACKER

David Packer takes the reader on a railway tour of this fascinating county. The varied photographs bear witness to the variety of steam, including pre-Grouping types, over the years. His captions set the images in context, ensuring that *Cheshire Steam* will appeal to anyone who remembers the era – bringing back many happy memories and providing a wealth of background detail.

978 0 7509 4678 0

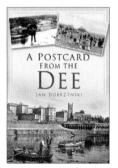

A Postcard from the Dee

JAN DOBRZYNSKI

The River Dee flows for over 70 miles through Wales and England to the Irish Sea. This book takes the reader on a pictorial journey, illustrated with over 200 old picture postcards from the author's extensive collection. It is a record of how the river once appeared to earlier generations of artists, writers and photographers. This is a stunning pictorial record of the whole length of the river, from source to sea, and an invaluable reference to locals, visitors and postcard collectors alike.

978 0 7509 5119 7

Visit our website and discover thousands of other History Press books.
www.thehistorypress.co.uk